MARKED
BY LOVE

Unveiling the Substance of Your True Identity

CATHERINE TOON, MD

Publishing, LLC

MARKED BY LOVE by Catherine Toon, MD
Published by Imprint Publishing
PO Box 63125 Colorado Springs, CO 80962-3125
United States

www.catherinetoon.com
Phone: (724) 677-6801
Email: info@catherinetoon.com

ISBN 978-0-692-84384-0 (Paperback Edition)
ISBN 978-0-692-84385-7 (Kindle Edition)

Library of Congress Control Number 2017905174

Printed in the United States of America
First Printing May 2017

Credits and Permissions:

Scripture taken from the Holy Bible, NEW INTERNATIONAL VERSION, NIV. Copyright 1973, 1978, 1984, 2011 by Biblica, Inc. Used by permission. All rights reserved worldwide.

Scripture quotations taken from the New American Standard Bible (NASB), Copyright 1960, 1962, 1963, 1968, 1971, 1972, 1973, 1975, 1977, 1995 by The Lockman Foundation. Used by permission. www.Lockman.org

Scripture quotations taken from the Amplified Bible (AMP), Copyright 2015 by The Lockman Foundation. Used by permission. www.Lockman.org

Scripture quotations taken from the Amplified Bible (AMPC), Copyright 1954, 1958, 1962, 1964, 1965, 1987 by The Lockman Foundation. Used by permission. www.Lockman.org

Scripture taken from the New King James Version. Copyright 1982 by Thomas Nelson. Used by permission. All rights reserved.

Scripture taken from The Voice. Copyright 2012 by Ecclesia Bible Society. Used by permission. All rights reserved.

Scripture taken from the King James Bible is Public domain and may be used freely, without restriction and without prior permission.

Scripture quotations are taken from the Holy Bible, New Living Translation, copyright 1996, 2004, 2007, 2013, 2015 by Tyndale House Foundation. Used by permission of Tyndale House Publishers, Inc., Carol Stream, Illinois 60188. All rights reserved.

Scripture quotations marked (TLB) are taken from The Living Bible copyright 1971. Used by permission of Tyndale House Publishers, Inc., Carol Stream, Illinois 60188. All rights reserved.

Verses listed without translation references are partially quoted or inferred.

Editing by Yeamah Logan, Grammargal (Fiverr), and Pamela Waldschmidt, Book Cover, Interior Design & Photography by Granite Pillar Media LLC, Graphic Design by Kelsey and David Chapman.

DEDICATIONS

To my wonderful husband, Brian – the love of my life:

Thank you for all the support you give day after day and your quiet confidence in me. You are an amazing husband and father. You are truly God's gift to me. I love doing life with you!

To my amazing children:

Beautiful Veronica – you are so pure and lovely and spread kindness wherever you go. You are such a joy to me and so many!

Relentless Rachel – you are so determined and refreshing with your cut-through-the-stuff voice. You are so gifted and beautiful in so many ways. I am so very, very proud of you!

Powerhouse Robert – you are truly one of a kind. You make me see through new eyes and laugh every day. You are awesome!

To my beautiful sister, Cassandra – you know me in ways no one else does! Thank you for your support and believing in me and your big-sister-bear protectiveness. I am so grateful God gave you to me!

To my mother, Inge – thank you so much for your support throughout my life and from heaven. Your love and beauty are constant. I sure miss you!

To my fabulous Team:

Rachel – you have such a servant's heart. I see kids, kids, and more kids. Thank you for the hours and hours that you have joyfully poured into Imprint in every area! You are truly a gift!

Amy – you are so uniquely beautiful inside and out; you light up the whole room with your smile and laugh. Thank you for your "Zoe" creativity and generosity!

Yeamah – you are the voice of "you can do it, so get her done!" I love your no-nonsense drive! Thank you for all the tireless editing/publishing input! You are truly a naked diamond!

To Schlyce – what can I say? Thank you so much for seeing, believing in, and empowering me! You have paid such a price to release the DMV of heaven ID cards, including mine! We have been through a heap together. I am so grateful for you and our friendship! The best is yet to come!

To Nate – you have helped me navigate through loss, emotional and relational crisis, and identity crisis. You are a gift to me and so many! Thank you for being such a wonderful friend!

To Mark Virkler – thank you so much for your support, suggestions, and permission to use "How to Hear God's Voice." You are such a dynamic instrument in the hand of the Lord to help the body commune intimately with God!

To God – I'm speechless. You take my breath away!

ENDORSEMENTS

"This beautiful volume by Catherine Toon is a devotional reading that aims to encourage you in your identity as created in the image of God and forever embraced and nurtured in His love. It reminds me of so many treatises by the early church mystics whose simple yet profound meditations on God's intimate communion bolster us in the depth of His sweet and tangible presence!"

John Crowder
Sons of Thunder Ministries & Publications

"I encourage you to read *Marked by Love* slowly. Let it sink in, then re-read it until it becomes a part of you. Look up the scripture verses and do the exercises. As you meditate on it and walk it out, it can radically change you into the person God created you to be. Catherine Toon's new book clearly shows you how to experience the reality of the Lord in your life, not just have an intellectual knowledge about Him. She shows you how to know who you are and why you are here — what your purpose in life is. I highly recommend this book as essential to understanding the Christian life!"

Gary Oates
Author *Open My Eyes, Lord*

"At first glance, this book might look like another generic book on the seemingly overdone topic of "love." Yet, I assure you, there is nothing generic, stale or overdone about this book! How can one read a book and understand God's love – I mean, truly "get" it? In this book, you will not read about love, you get to witness Love. Having overcome tremendous pain and insecurity herself, Catherine speaks from a depth of knowing and partaking in the love of God.

Catherine is genuinely infatuated with the personhood of God. Her exuberance jumps off the pages and gets all over you! It is so contagious, in fact, that you will feel whisked away into this giddy, spunky, irrational romance with her God of Love. Then, you will turn the page and find yourself crying as she drops a truth-bomb that hits your soul like a wrecking ball. As I read every sentence I felt led to slow down, to enter into another realm to let her words minister to my soul.

The Love Encounter Breaks are hidden gems in every chapter – simple and profound all at once. Don't skip a single one! Give yourself time to truly allow God to minister to your heart, touch deep areas of pain, and bring life and healing. Through her words and activations, Catherine shows you how to connect with and encounter God in a real and tangible way. Get ready to discover your true worth and identity, and fall in love with Love Himself!"

Karen Welton
Weltonacademy.com

"Catherine is prophetic in her experience and her writing style. God has done some powerful and amazing healing in her life and spirit.

Catherine shares this from her heart, with a passionate desire to see this same healing passed on to others."

Mark Virkler

President, Communion with God Ministries

"There was a day that I thought the message of God's love was 'milk,' and that knowledge and revelation was the meat, but the older that I have gotten I realize that love is the 'meat' of our walk with God. Paul tells us in Ephesians 3:19, 'that we may know the love of Christ which surpasses knowledge, that we may be filled with the fullness of God.' Knowing His fullness is knowing His love, and in the book *Marked by Love* Catherine Toon does an excellent job revealing the heart of that to us. I highly recommend this book to anyone that is desiring to know God in a fresh and powerful way by understanding our union with God who IS love. Catherine lives this message in her life and ministry, and anyone that has ever been around her can see and sense the fruit of her life being marked by love."

Bishop Jamie Englehart

Apostolic Overseer, Heritage International Ministries & Apostolic Resource Ministries

"Your words are so soothing and touching. I found myself getting lost in the pages as I felt a warm and calming feeling enter my body. This book is an exceptional idea."

Suzie Housley

Midwest Book Reviewer

"Oh, how I wish everyone could read this book. As a pastor, my heart's desire and passion is that people would grow and come up into the full stature of who they are in Christ; that they would become fully mature children of God. But the devil has carefully created a minefield to destroy us and keep us from becoming the beautiful creation God birthed and intended. Catherine Toon is giving the Body of Christ a real gift. This book lovingly invites and comfortably welcomes you into the Love of God and the Safe Place that He is; you'll miss the devil's minefield completely. After reading this book you'll realize that it's not only OK to be you, but it is required. You'll find a safe place in God with permission from Him to grow comfortably in an atmosphere of Love. I am often struck with wonder when I see Christians with real internal impediments, hindrances to their growth, and I wonder how that could be. While growing up I was actually accused of living in a 'bubble' because I was so protected, so blessed, so safe while those around me were suffering serious injury. While reading this book I realized that I experienced what Catherine is talking about all through my youth. I was maturing in an atmosphere of love. It's almost like Catherine is welcoming you into God's living room, showing you around, exploring all the details and aspects and wonder of it, then she tells you, 'This is your home. Welcome Home!'"

Joseph Barlow
Pastor, Family Life Christian Center
President, Joseph Barlow Ministries

"GOD IS LOVE. BY THIS THE LOVE OF GOD WAS IN US, THAT GOD HAS SENT HIS ONLY BEGOTTEN SON INTO THE WORLD SO THAT WE MIGHT LIVE THROUGH HIM."

1 JOHN 4:8-9 (NASB)

CONTENTS

FOREWORD

"WHAT THE WORLD NEEDS NOW IS LOVE, SWEET LOVE
IT'S THE ONLY THING THAT THERE'S JUST TOO LITTLE OF
WHAT THE WORLD NEEDS NOW IS LOVE, SWEET LOVE
NO, NOT JUST FOR SOME BUT FOR EVERYONE"
– HAL DAVID (LYRICS)

"WHOEVER DOES NOT LOVE DOES NOT KNOW GOD, BE-
CAUSE GOD IS LOVE."
– 1 JOHN 4:8

There's a huge vacuum in the heart of humanity and there's only one thing that will fill it – love. Love is the answer, the only answer to the cry of the human heart. But, what is love, really? How do you describe it? Is it something you fall in or out of? Is it a feeling you feel? Is it a choice you make? Is it a verb or noun? The definition of love in the dictionary leaves the most important part out. It doesn't mention God. It omits the central point.

God is Love, or stated as truly in reverse, Love is God. If you really want to understand love, you have to meet God. You have to get to know God. This is the reason *Marked by Love* is such a powerful book. Love is a person. He has a face. He has a voice. He has a heart.

As you read this book, you will meet Him, face to face. You will encounter the face of Love.

Like the Apostle Paul whose upbringing prepared him to take on the world, Catherine is uniquely qualified and gifted to write a book on the topic of love. As a survivor of childhood sexual abuse, her revelation of real love is revolutionary. Every page of *Marked by Love* carries an encounter with the One who loves you beyond your wildest imagination. It will revolutionize your concept of God, heal your relationship with yourself, and expand your capacity to love others.

I encourage you to really take your time as you read through this book. Allow its poetic tone to seduce your heart. Chew on the goodness of God that drips from each and every sentence. Pause and meditate on the scriptural truths that Catherine explains so eloquently. Permit the reality of your true identity as His beloved to sink in.

Take time to reflect on Catherine's personal stories and encounters with God. Each and every one is an opportunity for you to release your faith and receive an impartation for greater intimacy with God. And by all means, don't rush through the Love Encounter Breaks at the end of every chapter. Spend time basking in Love's delight. Look deep into the eyes of Love and allow Love's passion to saturate your entire being.

The experiences that you are about to embark on as you read *Marked by Love* are going to rock your world. It is an amazing book by an amazing woman. Catherine is uniquely gifted to help you encounter God's love. Her heart is as pure as it is powerful. As you read this book, expect to be transformed. Love is about to invade your life. You are about to fall deeper in love with Love.

Schlyce Jimenez
Founder and CEO,
Emerge School of Transformation
by Rethink, LLC

INTRODUCTION

Y ou were marked. You were marked by God. You were marked
by Love!

God is Love (1 John 4:8). Central to my mandate in most everything
I do, including writing this book, is to help you connect with God as
Love and connect with who you have been made to be in the image
of Love. Additionally, I am mandated to help you connect with your
purpose to reveal and be a conduit of Love and to be released and
empowered with that purpose. It is a process of unveiling and discovery. Love undergirds and is interlaced with the very reasons why
you were born on planet Earth.

It's time to encounter the God, Who placed you here. It's time to
encounter Love. And in doing so, you will encounter who God really
made you to be.

If your spiritual journey has stalled out or has never really gotten started, this book is for you. If you have fallen into a lot of joyless doing, there is something wrong. If your spiritual journey has been marked by striving to fill a void that won't be filled and won't stay filled, something is way off.

God is Love, and He is so chock full of Himself that He wants to fill you, overflow, and wreak Love havoc on a loveless, empty, chaotic world. And He wants to start and continue with YOU first.

This book carries encounters with the Person of Love. It carries the promise of encountering God with a "Do not pass go. Do not collect $200," until you get more of this ingrained in you. With that, I am believing that you will get new eyes or fresh eyes to see yourself from Love's perspective. And you will love what you see!

My job is to partner with God to help you get there from wherever you are at. There is always more to learn. There's always something more to experience. Love never gets old. It is never tired and worn out. It is always fresh and exciting and life-giving, because Love is God Himself.

Your job is to be willing, and to be willing to trust that God made you for this regardless of your personal experience. Give God your "expectors" and expect Him to lift them way up and not drop them. He is confident in His ability to speak the dialect of your love language! And I am totally confident in Him.

This book is a deep and high and joyous exploratory experiential romp in the expanse of Love. It is not a weighty, exhaustive theological discourse on God as love. That is not because I disdain stellar theological scholarship.

It is simply because when you are in love with someone, you delight to discover more and more about them. You can't objectively dissect, quantify, and put them in neat little boxes. That is partly because you are so distracted by the one you are enamored with and partly because of the futility of trying to figure out the magic of how God ticks. After a while you just have to settle down and just enjoy Him, and let Him enjoy you. Love doesn't fit in a box, no matter how big or well thought out it may be.

So keeping that in mind, be very clear – you are marked: You were marked before you were born. You were marked by God. You were marked by Love. God is Love (1 John 4:8, 16).

Love is a Person Who is motivated by Himself. When you are Love, you cannot help but love and do everything out of love to benefit and delight the one you love.

But be forewarned: This is not a tame treatise, because Love will not be confined. I fully expect Him to jump off the pages to envelop you. He might plant a big juicy kiss right on the lips. He might rest upon you so heavily that you think you might pass out. He might take you somewhere amazing in the Spirit. He might sweetly caress your hair or blow on you or whisper sweet somethings in your ear. You might think crazy fabulous "that was not me" thoughts. You might simply be drawn without a lot of evident supernatural angelic encounters. Love is a master woo-er. Love is not sedate. He is an endlessly hopeful romantic. He is unabashedly passionate, so all bets are off!

At the same time, He is also oh-so tender and protective! You can trust Him. He knows your story. He knows where you came from. He knows how to keep you safe. He knows where you are going and His plans for you. And He knows how to get you there from here.

Why am I qualified to write this book? I have spent A LOT of time encountering Love. I needed to.

In December of 2009, I was journaling and asking the Lord about why I was on the earth and the purpose for which I was born. He simply said, "You were born in love to love. You are an apostle of Love. Your mandate is to love...I have called you as witness to the body, but also as a witness to the world." That sounded pretty great, but frankly pretty freaky. I had to look up what apostle meant. I had images of stained glass windows and robed men. Being a "sent one" gave me images of envelopes and postage stamps.

But I do have a message. It is a message of a tangible God. It is a message of tangible Love. It is a message and a Person you were created for. It is all about you in the context and reality of full-blown unadulterated, undiluted Love.

Intermittently throughout this book, I have "Love Encounter Breaks" to get you out of reading and studying mode and into receiving and encountering mode. These are short, but you can take as long as you want. There is no quiz. There is no grade. There is no substandard encounter with Love.

There is no performance on your part, except giving yourself permission to let yourself encounter God as Love and receive what He wants to show you about yourself, made in that love. Give yourself ample opportunities to practice receiving – and believe God made you for encounters with Him. If you were brought up to believe that God is unknowable, you were misinformed. We will forever be growing in our knowledge of Him. But the point is to be growing, not to throw our hands up simply because He is God and too big to know fully.

Love wants to be known by the object of His love. In case you need some convincing and help with this, here are some non-exhaustive references in scripture that are all about knowing God: Psalm 16:10; Psalm 36:10; Psalm 67:1-3; Ephesians 1:8-10; Ephesians 1:17-19; Ephesians 3:2-4, 10; Ephesians 4:13; Philippians 3:8-10; Colossians 1:9-10; Colossians 3:10; 1 Timothy 2:3-5; Hebrews 8:11; 2 Peter 1:2-3, 5; 1 John 2:3-5; 1 John 2:20-21; 1 John 4:2, 6; 1 John 4:7-8, 13, 16.

Love wants to be known!

Because Love wants to be known, He interacts with His kids. God speaks and wants to be heard. You have the capacity to connect with God (Psalm 91:5; Psalm 40:6; Jeremiah 33:3; Isaiah 30:21; John 10:27; John 16:13; James 1:5-6).

Psalms 91:15 and Jeremiah 33:3 say that if you call on Him, He will answer you.

He interacts with His kids through their spiritual senses:

- Spiritual sight (Habakkuk 2:2; Acts 2:17; Ephesians 1:17-18)
- Spiritual hearing (Psalm 40:6; Isaiah 20:21; John 10:27)
- Spiritual touch (John 14:6; Romans 8:11)
- Spiritual taste (Psalm 34:8; Psalm 19:10)
- Spiritual smell (Song of Solomon 1:3; 2 Corinthians 2:13-16)

Each believer also has an "internal knowing" referred to as the inner witness (Romans 2:15; Romans 8:16) – God speaking from the inside out as just "knowing."

He also gives people His thoughts, which are referred to as the "mind of Christ" (1 Corinthians 2:16). It is pretty mind-blowing that you have access to Love's mind. Just make sure the parts that are blown away are the parts that are not thinking in line with what God is saying.

He also leads people through peace (Colossians 3:15).

Sometimes Love will send angels or cause supernatural signs and wonders (Matthew 1:20,24; Acts 5:19, 8:26, 9:36-42; Mark 16:20; 2 Kings 6:5; John 2:7-9). God also speaks through His word, and all things must line up with rightly divided scripture. If they do not, they must be tossed out. This is to protect us from error.

Remember, Love will keep you entirely safe (Psalm 91; Proverbs 1:33; 2 Timothy 1:12). Perfect Love casts out fear because perfect Love knows how to protect, heal, and nurture (1 John 4:18).

God is a God who wants to be known, and He will help you with that. That is why Holy Spirit, as Love, is called The Helper (John 14:16, 26; 15:26; 16:7). He is your Guide and will show you things to come (John 14:26; 16:13).

In your encounters, let Love do the heavy lifting (Matthew 11:28-30). Don't try too hard; He is really good at His job as a Teacher! You may receive a word or words, thoughts, pictures, feelings, impressions, a knowing, a scripture, or untold ways in which Love wants to manifest on your behalf. Since Love is God and He is Truth, He will always, without exception show Himself in line with the scripture He wrote about Himself (1 Corinthians 13:4-8; Galatians 5:22; 1 John 4:18; Hebrews 13:8; James 1:17).

So with that in mind, you can expect Love always to be unchangingly safe, patient, kind, you-centered, honoring, hard to offend, forgiving (and forgetting past offenses). He is good (the way a four-year-old would say is good), full of truth, trusting and trustworthy, hopeful, joyful, peaceful, faithful, gentle, and self-controlled.

As you read through, I suggest that you do the "Love Encounter Breaks" as you come to them. If you have to skip them as you read, I recommend that you go back and do them later to get the full juiciness of each one.

Dr. Mark Virkler, president of Communion with God Ministries, generously offered his superb "How to Hear God's Voice" resource, which I included verbatim (see Appendix B) to help you grow in your ability to connect with the Lord. For those of you who connect with God primarily in your thoughts, Mark's resource will particularly be a boon for you. But regardless of your primary way of connecting to Him, it will be a huge blessing. Thank you, Mark!

I also recommend that you get a journal (a regular notebook is fine) so that you have lots of space and privacy to write down what you are getting. This will be invaluable: Love will "speak" to you, and you will want to record it and go back to it!

In Appendix C I included a personal two-way journal entry, a conversation between me and the Lord, about what He wants you to know about Who He is for you and what that means for you specifically as the *Marked By Love* audience. This will give you an idea of what two-way journaling between you and the Lord can look like, understanding that your journaling will look distinctly like you and

Him. Your relationship with Love will come alive as you practice two-way journaling regularly.

I have already prayed over all of you for the complete safety, ease, and impactfulness of your encounters. But I will pray again in writing so you can absorb it:

> *Pappa, I thank You that You love Your kids so much that You want them close and to know Your heart for them and who You have made them to be specifically and uniquely. I thank You for jumping off the pages as they go through this book, and I thank You for being tangible to each and every person right where and how they need it in each of the Love Encounter breaks. I thank You for enlightening the eyes of their imaginations, for all Your kids' spiritual senses to be awakened, heightened, and trained in discernment. I thank You that only Your agendas will be accomplished throughout this book and in all the Love Encounter Breaks. In the name and through the blood of Jesus Christ, I forbid any hindrances, harassment, and assignments of any masquerading by spirits who were not born in the flesh of a virgin, who did not die for the sins of the entire world on the cross, who were not raised on the third day and seated at the right hand of the Father. I thank You, Holy Spirit, for leading each and every person into the Truth of Who You, Jesus, and Father God are as Love. I thank You for heaven invading earth right here, right now, right where each and every person is at. I thank You for Your fruit abounding. I thank You for power released in Your Love and that each and every person will walk away beautifully and powerfully transformed. And I give You all the glory and honor and the praise – You rock! In Jesus's name, amen!*

So buckle up your seatbelts! You were marked by Love. It's time to encounter God. It's time to encounter Love. And it is time to encounter yourself from Love's perspective.

And that is my prayer and heart for you!

– Catherine

1.

THE EPICENTER OF THE UNIVERSE

The Meaning of Life

The meaning of life...Poets, the church, science, educators, the entertainment industry, the financial industry, our parents, our friends, and all different segments of societies throughout the ages have grappled with this. The existentialist says there is no meaning. The narcissist says it is "all about me." The martyr says it is "all about everyone else." Religion says it is all about doing good or being spiritual. The hedonist says it is all about pleasure.

No wonder we are so confused, anxious, depressed, and exhausted! God, as Creator of us and the universe, has a lot to say on the matter. Life without Him, as God's Word says, under the sun, IS meaning-

less. Love brings meaning and context to everything in life whether
it is pain or pleasure. Love is a Person. Life without Him is empty:

> *The words of the Teacher, son of David, king in Jerusalem: "Mean-*
> *ingless! Meaningless!" says the Teacher. "Utterly meaningless! Ev-*
> *erything is meaningless." (Ecclesiastes 1:1-2 NIV)*

Most people agree that they need something bigger than themselves
for meaning. Try as we might to find the next fulfilling thing, at the
end of the day, anything less than God is not big enough. It's like the
vegetarian platter on a Chinese food menu. It may be great while it
lasts, but then you're hungry an hour later.

God gives meaning and context to
everything. Love fills the nagging
void that we often can't even identify
but try to medicate with all our med-
ications of choice.

At the end of the day, we were designed to need love so intrinsically
and so endlessly that only God can
fill it. A life without love is empty
and void.

WE WERE
DESIGNED TO
NEED LOVE SO
INTRINSICALLY
AND SO
ENDLESSLY
THAT ONLY
GOD CAN FILL
IT.

All people love imperfectly, because they are not the Source of love.
They are the recipients of Love. You can love only as well as you have
received Love. And there is only one perfect Source. That Source

gives meaning to everything "under the sun" (Ecclesiastes 1:1-3; 12:13).

So what is the deal with God? He's big – He fills everything with Himself. The universe cannot contain Him. He's good and holy – better than we can dare ask, think, hope, or dream. He's powerful, even upholding all things by the word of His power. He's wise, with unfathomable glorious riches. He is peace, upholding governance of His expanding Kingdom. We need all of the above. They provide the meaning we all require.

Since He is God, I think He gets to define Himself, and He did so.

God is love (1 John 4:8; 4:16).

The Person of Love

Love is a person Who is motivated by Himself. When you are Love, you cannot help but love and do everything out of love.

Marked by Love is a deep and high and joyous exploration of the expanse of God, Who is Love. How do you begin to grasp the hugeness of God? You start from where you are at and keep going. It is a project of eternity that becomes more fascinating as you go! If you have gotten bored with God, you have gotten disconnected with the most fascinating, intoxicating Person in the universe. You have gotten hoodwinked into thinking that something He created might be more satisfying than its Creator. He's not mad at you for this, but He wants to lovingly call you back into the freshness of first love! And He is not looking for *you* to muster love up.

He will lovingly give you the grace to help you back into divine romance with Him!

I am fully persuaded that Love is the person, but also the primary nature of God. Yes, He is holy. But nowhere in the Bible does it say, God is holiness. The word of God does say He is our righteousness.

He is also the Spirit of wisdom and understanding, as well as counsel and might and knowledge:

> *The Spirit of the Lord will rest on Him, The spirit of wisdom and understanding, The spirit of counsel and strength, The spirit of knowledge and the fear of the Lord. (Isaiah 11:2 NASB)*

IF YOU HAVE GOTTEN BORED WITH GOD, YOU HAVE GOTTEN DISCONNECTED WITH THE MOST FASCINATING, INTOXICATING PERSON IN THE UNIVERSE.

As you search out scripture, you see over and over again that His primary nature is relational. He is Father. He is Husband. He is Friend. He is Love. Love is both Who He is and the motivation behind everything He has done and is doing. You can surely say God is self-motivated.

Love - The Epicenter of the Universe

Love is the epicenter of the universe, and He inhabits and fills every nook and cranny of it (Ephesians 1:23; 4:10).

Psalm 139 (NKJV) says that God not only is everywhere (omnipresent), but He is even in hell. Since hell is commonly defined as separation from God, that messes with pet theology. But here it is in black and white:

> *Where can I go from Your Spirit? Or where can I flee from Your presence? If I ascend into heaven, You are there; If I make my bed in hell, behold, You are there. If I take the wings of the morning, And dwell in the uttermost parts of the sea, Even there Your hand shall lead me, And Your right hand shall hold me. If I say, 'Surely the darkness shall fall on me,' Even the night shall be light about me; Indeed, the darkness shall not hide from You, But the night shines as the day; The darkness and the light are both alike to You.*

How can people be in hell when Love is there? I believe that people who insist on rejecting Christ and what Love purchased out of love are tormented in the very same fires of Love, that warm and bring life and joy to those who embrace Him.

The word of God says Love upholds all things by His powerful word (Hebrews 1:3). As the epicenter of the universe, Love is the power that upholds everything. And He does it by His words. That means when God says it, something happens. He has no impotent or flabby words. In Genesis 1, God was busy creating the world that we see.

He said, "Light be!" and shaka-bam, there was light (Genesis 1:3).
He divided it and named it and it was good (Genesis 1:4-5). He
spoke everything else we see into existence. That is power, my friend,
and there is a lot we can learn by speaking as sons and daughters of
Love to release love!

Love has also framed the worlds by the word of His power (Hebrews 11:3). I know he has totally framed and saturated my world.

And because Love is so infinite, the universe has to keep on expanding because it cannot contain Him.

Love is the epicenter, the alpha and omega, the beginning and end, and every letter in between.

Love created everything in love; that is why He said everything He created was so good. But when He created humankind, He outdid Himself (proud Pappa). That, He said, was *very* good (Genesis 1:31).

> BECAUSE LOVE IS SO INFINITE, THE UNIVERSE HAS TO KEEP ON EXPANDING BECAUSE IT CANNOT CONTAIN HIM.

It is interesting that the first thing Love created was light. Love indeed lights up the universe.

The word of God says that God is Light (John 8:12; 9:5) and the Father of Lights in Whom there is no shadow of turning (James 1:17). God is Love and is the epicenter of the universe. God is Light, and so Light must be the epicenter as well. In a very real sense, Love is the epicenter of the universe and lights up that universe with Himself.

Love lights the way and is The Way (John 8:12; 9:5, 2; 14:6; Corinthians 4:4)!

Psalm 139:12 (NLT) says,

> *But even in darkness I cannot hide from you. To you the night shines as bright as day. Darkness and light are the same to you. The darkness and the light are both alike to You.*

Loving the Entire World

Love chose to buy back the entire world before He even created it (Revelation 13:8).

John 3:16-17 (NIV) says (emphasis added),

> *For God so loved the world that he gave his one and only Son, that whoever believes in him shall not perish but have eternal life. For God did not send his Son into the world to condemn the world, but to **save the world** through him.*

First John 2:2 (NIV) (emphasis added) also says,

> *He is the atoning sacrifice for our sins, and not only for ours but also for the sins of the **whole world.***

Quite singlehandedly He has the whole world covered. The problem is the world does not know it. Many believers aren't quite sure either, for that matter! And they needlessly struggle with the torment of condemnation that Jesus bore for them (Romans 8:1; Isaiah 53:5). Much of the body of Christ, if not most, are confused about the nature of God and so have misrepresented Him as a "nice, but watch-out" God.

Jesus said in John 12:47(NIV),

> *If anyone hears my words but does not keep them, I do not judge that person. For I did not come to judge the world, but to save the world.*

So much of the body of Christ lives with this ongoing sense that in God's eyes they just do not measure up. The truth is that God measured His Son and placed you in Him, placed Him in you, and made you one with Him (1 Corinthians 6:17; Romans 8:1; 6:3-4).

Love has done a sweeping work, and He wants EVERYONE to know it! No one is outside the parameters of Love. Am I a Universalist? Only to the extent that Love is universal. And it just doesn't look like our Western evangelical formulas. If someone insists on rejecting Love, what they experience will be torment. Fear in whatever flavor, from restlessness to terror and panic, is tormenting. First John 4:18 says that perfect love casts out fear. And the reason Love comes as an antidote to fear is that Love simply won't have His beloved tormented. When Love has you and Love is powerful on your behalf, why would you need to fear?

LOVE HAS DONE A SWEEPING WORK, AND HE WANTS EVERYONE TO KNOW IT! NO ONE IS OUTSIDE THE PARAMETERS OF LOVE.

Perfect Love is a Person Who simply eradicates fear because He is so big and good and personal and powerful. Love never fails (1 Corinthians 13:8).

Faith is what releases God's power on the earth realm. The word of God says that faith works by love (Galatians 5:6). When you are connected to Love, your faith works and the power of God can flow!

It is the goodness of God that draws all men to change their thinking (repentance) to embrace the One Who loves them (Romans 2:4)! Love is unabashedly sneaky. And He doesn't apologize for covert or overt tactics – whatever it takes.

Love is relentlessly pursuing you! He is relentlessly pursuing the entire world.

Annoying Relentless Love

In my own story, I had had early, rather dramatic encounters with the Lord, although I had no clue it was Jesus. I am not sure I heard the term *Gospel* until I was in my early teens. And then I had no clue what the Gospel was. It was one of those weird terms used by those even weirder Christian people.

Because I was living in the reality of sexual abuse and a lack of love, affirmation, and security, I learned the lie that something clearly must be wrong with me. The unwritten rule at some level stemming from some of my family was that people were objects to be used, if they were noticed at all. The thing that made you valued was what you did, not who you were. I became a performer academically and high-brow culturally, which was what was prized in our home. I turned my back on much of my own heart, which hurt too much. I turned my back on anything having to do with Jesus – that was *not* prized in our home.

As our family continued to disintegrate, I became more and more angry at God. If He was so big and so powerful, why would He stand by and let everything I cared about be destroyed? I was not receptive to all the people He kept on sending to me or the situations He orchestrated pointing toward His goodness and His love. Even though I was prospering as a physician in-training at high-powered institutions, the wreckage inside began to catch up and overtake me on the outside. I had one failed marriage and then a series of from bad to worse relationships (read "stupid with no boundaries") that left me more broken and ashamed. I started having flashbacks of the sexual abuse that I had buried alive and wouldn't stay buried. I was in professionally functional but personally "I-am-not-strong-enough-to handle-this-chaos" mode. Jesus had still been pursuing me HARD in the midst.

When I was twenty-seven, He finally wore me down. Everywhere I turned, there He was – so kind and patient and annoying. But I was also secretly grateful. I really WANTED all those good things about a God of Love to be true. I just hadn t experienced them. More on all that later. When you are running from God with a big chip on your shoulder, you don't want to see Him. You don't want to talk to Him even if He is really the only One Who can help you.

The modus operandi (MO) of the enemy of our souls is all about stealing, killing, and destroying (John 10:10). And he loves it when he is successful and then we turn around and blame the One, Who only has good for us and is the only One Who can truly help us. satan wants you offended and functionally separate from God because of that offense. He wants you to blame God for his (satan's) havoc in your life. He wants to represent God as a liar, Who is not there for you or Who is passive and impotent. He paints God as Someone Who is impossible to please and Who is a nice guy one minute and wrathful and unpredictable the next. He wants you to see God as out there somewhere in the vast expanse, uninvolved and disinterested, unknowable and repulsed by your weaknesses and struggles. He brands God as Someone Who rejects His kids, if He even notices them. Satan wants you to see God like the people who yielded to his evil. Ask me how I know! If you think God looks like any of that mess, you are not going to be too responsive when He comes knocking on the door of your heart.

Life with God is hard. Life without God is unimaginable to me now. God really IS LOVE. All pure, unadulterated love stems from Him. Love is relentless: melting hard hearts, warming cold hearts, thawing frozen hearts, and resurrecting dead hearts.

> LOVE IS MASTERFUL AND CONFIDENT IN HIS ABILITY TO WOO AND WIN EVEN THE HARDEST OF HEARTS.

Love is the epicenter and the expansion of the universe. And He has forgotten no one and has missed none of the details of His beloved creation. He is not concerned about His reputation. He is not concerned about the bad press from a fallen world with so much sin at the hands of people who confess His name. Love's branding problem can initially make people fearful, annoyed, or resistant to His advances. But He is masterful and confident in His ability to woo and win even the hardest of hearts.

I am often amused when I talk to person after person, each of whom is convinced that they or their loved ones are the hardest nuts to crack. Love is masterful with all kinds of hearts: hard hearts, dense hearts, sinful hearts, unbelieving hearts, cynical hearts, wounded hearts, shattered hearts, prideful hearts, fearful hearts – you name it! He's in the heart business.

He's been at work before there was a world, redeeming the whole kit and caboodle and swallowing it all up in Himself at the cross (1 Corinthians 15:28; Colossians 1:20).

Love has marked the world (Colossians 1:16).

Marked?

So what about this marked business? A mark is an imprint or impression that may be temporary, semi-permanent, or permanent. I was practicing medicine back in the day when tattoos were considered sort of cheap. So I'd see people get tattoos and then I'd see them regret them and have to go to great lengths and cost to get the tattoo faded or removed. Tattoos are pretty permanent, even if they do fade and stretch. God says you are tattooed on His very body:

> [And the Lord answered] Can a woman forget her nursing child, that she should not have compassion on the son of her womb? Yes, they may forget, yet I will not forget you. Behold, I have indelibly imprinted (tattooed a picture of) you on the palm of each of My hands; [O Zion] your walls are continually before Me (Isaiah 49:15-17 AMPC).

Apparently, you must be a pretty big deal. Love didn't tattoo you on His forehead or chest. He tattooed you on His palms so He could look at you with delight all the time! I can imagine God showing off in heaven, stretching out His palms to brag on you like a proud pappa popping out baby pictures.

The word says "indelibly." That means He doesn't go to the heavenly laser center to get your picture removed from His palms when you rebel, act out, or forget Him on His birthday.

Quite simply, YOU have marked Him, and He's delighted about it!

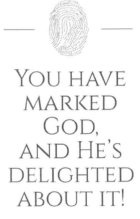

But let's look at the flipside of the equation: YOU have been marked. *You* have been *indelibly* marked. You have been indelibly marked by *Love*, Himself.

YOU HAVE MARKED GOD, AND HE'S DELIGHTED ABOUT IT!

What does that mean? I am so glad you asked! Whatever has impact leaves a mark – an imprint or impression.

God created you, and He didn't create you to look like a flower or stallion or an angel. He created you in His image and likeness (Genesis 1:26). Before God formed you, He knew all about you and the amazing plans He had for you (Jeremiah 1:5; 29:11; Psalm 139:13-17; Galatians 1:15-16).

Because you are a creation of Love, you are intrinsically marked by Love. A master artist not only signs his or her work in the lower right-hand corner, but with every stroke, every application of their media, every mix of hue, every blend and shade. The artist is intimately reflected in his or her work.

God didn't just zap you into the womb with a random sperm and egg. He knit you together and embroidered you as His masterpiece. The very substance of your being was created and birthed out of Him. He put His mark in your DNA when He chose which unique complement to give you, which genes to express and suppress, and how and when to express them. You are His orchestral symphonic masterpiece. You are like no other:

- The exact hue of your eyes
- The color of your hair and the way it falls
- The shade and texture of your skin
- Your smile and shape of your teeth
- Your eyebrows and lashes
- Your fingers and nail shapes
- Your finger and toe prints
- The way you laugh
- The tenor of your voice
- Your temperament
- The way you think, process, and relate to the world around you
- Your talents and strengths
- Your type of creativity

- And so on and so on and so on

And everything He did in Love. He never jostled over anyone in an assembly line because He was in a bad mood or was bored or distracted! He broke the mold after He made you, because any replications of His masterpiece would be an insult to the original.

You were made in love. You were chosen in love. You were formed and fashioned in Love. Love permeates the very essence of your being (Ephesians 1:3-6; Psalms 139:13-17). You have definitely, definatively been marked!

So you have to become a student of Love to really understand your makeup and what makes your authentic self tick.

This is why Paul prayed for strength that you could apprehend (get) Love! He doesn't just want you to know *about* Love; He wants you to *experience* Him as Love.

May He grant you out of the riches of His glory, to be strengthened and spiritually energized with power through His Spirit in your inner self, [indwelling your innermost being and personality], so that Christ may dwell in your hearts through your faith. And may you, having been [deeply] rooted and [securely] grounded in love, be fully capable of comprehending with all the saints (God's people) the width and length and height and depth of His love [fully experiencing that amazing, endless love]; and [that you may come] to know [practically, through personal experience] the love of Christ which far surpasses [mere] knowledge [without experience], that you may be filled up [throughout your being] to all the fullness of God [so that you may have the richest experience of God's presence in your lives, completely filled and flooded with God Himself]. (Ephesians 3:16-19 AMP)

That requires supernatural empowerment to get revelation. That is my prayer for you right now!

Love Encounter Break #1

Let's take a "selah" (a pause, crescendo, or musical interlude) to let some of that sink in! This is not a race to finish the book, but a luxurious journey into the heart of Love Himself to show you who you really are. If you skipped the introduction where I explain how best to approach this, now is the time to review it.

Let me pray this over you – just receive.

> *Pappa, I agree with the one reading this right now for the grace to rest and receive from You! You made them in Love. And although all of us tend to forget, You love to remind us of that love that defines every aspect of our truest selves. So right now I ask that You show this one in a word or words, thoughts, pictures, feelings, impressions, a knowing, or however else You want to manifest how You loved them and made them in Love before the foundation of the world. Show them at least one way that You marked them in Love.*

Now let yourself relax and let Love speak in those words, thoughts, pictures, feelings, impressions, knowings, or other manifestations. Jot down anything you are getting, however small, even if you are not sure it is God. You can review this later or bring it to a trusted spiritual leader to help you judge it.

Relax and let God do the heavy lifting. Let Him surprise you. Be patient with yourself if this is new. He will help you! You will get better and better at this as you practice!

If you need more space, grab or make a new journal.

How Love made His mark on me:

_____

_____

_____

_____

_____

_____

_____

_____

_____

_____

_____

_____

_____

_____

_____

_____

_____

_____

2.
THE FLAVORS
OF GOD

31 Flavors

When I was a little girl we would occasionally go to the ice cream store – you probably know the one – 31 flavors. I would peer over the display cases and contemplate each and every flavor. Sometimes the server would ask if I wanted a sample. After getting over my shyness, I would say, "Yes!" – and sample the delectable sweetness lingering over that pink plastic spoon. I had the fantasy of being let loose with a couple hundred of my closest friends, with unlimited spoons and samplings. We would spend hours debating the pros and cons of each flavor and rank each and every one. I could still go for that particular fantasy, spoons in hand, but I don't go very often. I like the ice cream, but it doesn't like me back – how rude!

I have been meditating on all that sampling. God is a God Who wants us to sample His goodness, with unlimited samplings. He even said, "Taste and see that (I am) good!" (Psalms 34:8).

I like the Message version:

> *Open your mouth and taste, open your eyes and see how good God is. Blessed are you who run to him.*

So let's grab our spoons and get going!

God is a God of limitless flavors, and there is not a bad one in the lot. Romans 11:33-36 in the Message version of the Bible says:

LOVE WANTS US TO SAMPLE HIS GOODNESS, WITH UNLIMITED SAMPLINGS.

> *Have you ever come on anything quite like this extravagant generosity of God, this deep, deep wisdom? It's way over our heads. We'll never figure it out. Is there anyone around who can explain God? Anyone smart enough to tell him what to do? Anyone who has done him such a huge favor that God has to ask his advice? Everything comes from him; Everything happens through him; Everything ends up in him. Always glory! Always praise! Yes. Yes. Yes.*

Despite His infiniteness, God is a God Who wants to be known by His kids and His Bride and His friends. Because our finite brains boggle quickly at His fathomless nature, He accommodates us

LOVE IS A PERSON WHO WANTS TO BE KNOWN.

where we are at. He gives us His mind by faith (1 Corinthians 2:16). Holy Spirit helps us to unwrap and sample flavor after flavor of His goodness. He is a relational God first and foremost, because He is Love. And He wants to be known by the objects of His desire.

Loveology

Theology is the study of God. "Loveology," as I am defining it, is the study of God as Love. You have to study something to know it. Love is a Person with many flavors, Who wants to be known. Everything is released through the knowledge of God.

Love's grace and peace are released through the knowledge of Him. The Classic Amplified version says that grace and peace are not only released but they are multiplied over and over and over through the knowledge of Love:

> *May grace (God's favor) and peace (which is perfect well-being, all necessary good, all spiritual prosperity, and freedom from fears and agitating passions and moral conflicts) be multiplied to you in [the full, personal, precise, and correct] knowledge of God and of Jesus our Lord. (2 Peter 1:2)*

That knowledge, however, is the word from the Greek *ep-ig-no-sis* meaning "recognition, full discernment, and acknowledgment." God was never meant to just be studied. God wants to be tasted. He wants to be experienced.

Love is so vast that He requires empowerment by His own Spirit of wisdom to reveal Himself and all His flavors (Ephesians 1:17). The Love of Christ is so vast it cannot be known just by our intellectual faculties, it requires intimate experiential encounters.

Knowing Love requires supernatural empowerment to taste and savor its flavors.

The Voice translation says the following in Ephesians 3:16-19:

> *Father, out of Your honorable and glorious riches, strengthen Your people. Fill their souls with the power of Your Spirit so that through faith the Anointed One will reside in their hearts. May love be the rich soil where their lives take root. May it be the bedrock where their lives are founded so that together with all of Your people they will have the power to understand that the love of the Anointed is infinitely long, wide, high, and deep, surpassing everything anyone previously experienced. God, may Your fullness flood through their entire beings.*

That knowledge and understanding is the Greek word *ginōskō*, which carries the idea of knowledge, understanding, and perception with such an intimate meaning that it carries the weight of a Jewish idiom for sexual intercourse between a man and a woman.

Truly, love does not blush! Love is naked and unashamed and infinitely accessible to the world He gave Himself up for. He had to take care of the sin issue so that He could be reconciled back to the entire world.

Will the Real God Stand Up?

God wants to be known. We can be sure of this because the whole of scripture is one unfolding after the next of Who God is. His true nature was veiled by the limitations of the covenants He had to move through.

> LOVE IS NAKED AND UNASHAMED AND INFINITELY ACCESSIBLE TO THE WORLD HE GAVE HIMSELF UP FOR.

God is a relational God first. He has always been in pursuit of humankind. In the garden, He was the One Who walked with Adam. He wasn't demanding worship. He wasn't creating rules to keep so that they could stay on good terms. He wanted fellowship. Even when Adam and his wife (later to be named Eve) fell, God's first response was "Where are you?" (Genesis 3:8-9, NIV):

> *Then the man and his wife heard the sound of the Lord God as he was walking in the garden in the cool of the day, and they hid from the Lord God among the trees of the garden. But the Lord God called to the man, "Where are you?"*

Adam's response:

He answered, "I heard you in the garden, and I was afraid because I was naked; so I hid."

This is the first time there was fear and separation and shame. Up until then, they had no clue they were naked. This is the first time Adam and Eve ever had any experience that was not grounded in Love.

God's next response was this:

And he said, "Who told you that you were naked? Have you eaten from the tree that I commanded you not to eat from?"

He had never intended that humankind ever be uncovered and outside of the full covering of Love. It was only then that the question of sin came up. God set about unfolding the plan He had made before the foundation of the world (Revelation 3:8) to cover this disaster.

Notice how the perception of God shifted with the fall. God was seen before the fall as a God of Love that we stand before and walk with totally naked – fully known and fully loved and accepted. This God made us to have loving dominion over everything but one another and to care for everything as we expanded His garden (Genesis 1:26-28).

After the fall, fear and shame entered. Now God was seen as someone to hide from. And the human race has been hiding ever since, because we have not seen Him rightly.

The word of God says God's true nature has been veiled (2 Corinthians 4:3-4; 23:13-16).

GOD'S TRUE NATURE HAS BEEN VEILED.

Jesus came as the express image of the Father (Hebrews 1:3) and died on the cross so that a new covenant of forgiveness could be established through his death, burial, and resurrection. That New Covenant makes it possible for a veil to be lifted off of people's hearts. That veil is the Law or the Covenant of Moses that has conned people into believing the lie that God's heart requires them to earn their own righteousness with endless dos and don'ts.

Second Corinthians 4:3 in the New International Version says the following:

And even if our gospel is veiled, it is veiled to those who are perishing. The god of this age has blinded the minds of unbelievers, so that they cannot see the light of the gospel that displays the glory of Christ, who is the image of God. For what we preach is not ourselves, but Jesus Christ as Lord, and ourselves as your servants for Jesus's sake. For God, who said, "Let light shine out of darkness," made his light shine in our hearts to give us the light of the knowledge of God's glory displayed in the face of Christ.

Notice that the light of the knowledge of God was displayed in the face of Jesus Christ. How many people have seen the Father as stern and angry but powerful, and Jesus as kind but perhaps wimpier? However, the word of God says that Jesus was the *exact representation* of the Father (Hebrews 1:3 NIV):

> *The Son is the radiance of God's glory and the exact representation of his being, sustaining all things by his powerful word.*

The old Covenant or Law veiled the goodness of God – a relational God who has always been in hot pursuit of people. The Law always demands, but never supplies. Love, on the other hand, supplied all the demand and has given the believer a paid-for gift of righteousness so that He could have a full, unhindered relationship with you!

If your toddler falls in the sewer, you dive in to fish them out and clean them up. You don't yell at them for being so stupid to fall in there and demand that they get themselves right back up and clean up their mess! God never expects anyone to fish themselves out and clean themselves up. That is a God-job! But, with that said, it is still smart to stay away from sewers!

LOVE NEVER EXPECTS ANYONE TO FISH THEMSELVES OUT AND CLEAN THEMSELVES UP. THAT IS A GOD-JOB!

Unfortunately, the church, in their zeal to be good and serve God, has often become hyper-focused and, frankly, scared of sin. And whatever you focus on and create rules to avoid becomes magnified and empowered, putting everyone in deeper bondage (1 Corinthians 15:56).

This is a real problem because now, not only is there the intrinsic destructiveness of sin, but a sin-consciousness and condemnation about that sin that make it impossible to overcome it.

But the word of God says that the reconciliation of the human race to God has been completely, utterly, and irrevocably taken care of on the cross:

> *You see, at just the right time, when we were still powerless, Christ died for the ungodly. But God demonstrates his own love for us in this: While we were still sinners, Christ died for us. Since we have now been justified by his blood, how much more shall we be saved from God's wrath through him! For if, while we were God's enemies, we were reconciled to him through the death of his Son, how much more, having been reconciled, shall we be saved through his life! Not only is this so, but we also boast in God through our Lord Jesus Christ, through Whom we have now received reconciliation. (Romans 5:6, 8-11 NIV)*

Sin is a huge issue in that it results in stealing, death, and destruction. And God hates sin because it does these things to His kids and it gives access to the enemy of our souls to run rampant. Sin may be covered, but yielding or diving into it still is stupid.

Jesus's sacrifice was not one for a few "good" people, but for the entire world to bring all things back to the Godhead (1 John 2:2 NIV, emphasis added):

> *He is the atoning sacrifice for our sins, and not only for ours but also for the sins of the **whole world.***

Colossians 1:19-2 in the New International Version (emphasis added) says:

> *For God was pleased to have all his fullness dwell in him, and through him to reconcile to himself **all things**, whether things on earth or things in heaven, by making peace through his blood, shed on the cross.*

Much of the church has operated from an old covenant mindset while preaching grace. It has focused on sin – as if Jesus did not do a good enough job and somehow we need to and are able to clean ourselves up. This has misrepresented God.

No one is drawn to condemnation – that is not good news! That is not the Gospel.

LOVE DELIGHTS IN US, RIGHT HERE, RIGHT NOW – YES, EVEN WITH OUR BIG HOT MESS!

The truth is, God did not want anything to come between Him and the entire human race and He became sin itself (2 Corinthians 5:21) so that we could be given His righteousness. He delights in us, right here, right now – yes, even with our big hot mess! He is there to help, not to condemn. He is there to pull us up into the righteous creation that He designed.

Conflicted Flavors

There has been a trend recently with making jellybeans with really funky, if not downright gross, flavors that look like the "good flavors." Check these out:

- Dead Fish – Strawberry Banana Smoothie
- Spoiled Milk – Coconut
- Stinky Socks – Tutti-Frutti
- Lawn Clippings – Lime
- Rotten Egg – Buttered Popcorn
- Toothpaste – Berry Blue
- Barf – Peach
- Canned Dog Food – Chocolate Pudding

That pretty much sums up the way so many of us have seen God.

- Angry – Forgiving
- Disappointed – Helping
- Wimpy - Peaceful
- Disinterested – Powerful
- Distant - Good
- Changeable – Merciful

- Correcting by bringing trials – Teaching
- Scary – Big

You get the picture. The problem when we have such confusion with how we see God is that *we* end up really conflicted. We want God to be close, just not too close. We want His help, but we are just not so sure that He will show up. We say He is faithful, but then are not so sure that we have performed enough for Him to back us up.

The common denominator for all the yucky hints of flavors is that they all bring fear. Fear undermines our faith. As a matter of fact, the word of God says that faith works by love (Galatians 5:6). I like the classic Amplified version that says that faith is activated and energized and expressed and working through love.

> FAITH IS A SIMPLE BELIEVING IN AND CONFIDENCE IN LOVE AND HIS GOODNESS TOWARD US.

Faith is a simple believing in and confidence in God and His goodness toward us. When faith is working, we can simply enjoy all the goodies (grace) that being a son/daughter of God provides. And we get that by inheritance, not striving (Romans 4:16; 5:6). If a child has to strive for their parents' approval, provision, protection, love, and inheritance, that is an abusive parent.

But it is really hard to trust a dad who is nice most of the time, but may turn around any minute with a fit of rage or disappointment. How can you count on a daddy who is so kind and merciful, but feels like a doddering old man who might need you to find his cane for him?

LOVE IS MASTERFUL AT HIS JOB, AND HE WANTS YOU TO KNOW HIM.

Just throwing scripture at our hearts does not always convince our hearts of the truth. We need an *encounter* with the Truth.

We need to see God rightly. Rightly dividing the Word of God is non-negotiable. However, just throwing scripture at our hearts does not always convince our hearts of the truth. We need an encounter with the Truth. We need encounters with Love. If this is you (pretty much a no-brainer), ask Him and let Him design what you are needing. He is a better Father than you are a child. He is a better Teacher than you are a student. He is a better Doctor than you are a patient. Let Him be God. Love is masterful at His job, and He wants you to know Him.

Love Encounter Break #2

Let's take a break to encounter Love and have Him reveal where your heart image of Him is conflicted.

> *Pappa, I agree with the one reading this right now for the grace to rest and receive from You! You made them in Love, but love has not always been present, or love has been confused, unpredictable, withheld, or perverted. Bad stuff has happened. So right now I ask that You show this one reading in a word or words, thoughts, pictures, feelings, impressions, a knowing, or however else You want to manifest how there has been distortion with Who You really are. I thank You that You are in the midst of the process and, if they need more help, You will help connect them exactly with the safe, effective help they need.*

Now let yourself relax, and let Love speak in those words, thoughts, pictures, feelings, impressions, knowings, or other manifestations, where He didn't feel present or didn't really feel like love. Jot down anything you are getting, however small, even if you are not sure it is God. You can review this later or bring it to a trusted spiritual leader to help you judge it.

How God has not looked or felt like love for me (These are lies that feel like truth):

_____

_____

_____

_____

_____

_____

You may well have to forgive some people or many people (i.e., God, your parents, your siblings, a teacher, an abuser, a church leader, the church in general, yourself). Know that you are not saying that the offense was in any way OK. Know that you are not doing this because they deserve to be forgiven. Know that you don't have to reconcile with the person/people if you are not ready or they are simply unsafe. You are just releasing the toxic tie to the offense that is poisoning you, not them. This is about your freedom from the offense and clearing away hindrances to connecting with Love, the only One Who can really heal and help you!

Let me pray:

> *Pappa, please bring up in the mind of the one reading this, anyone they need to release in forgiveness. Thank You for the grace to do the hard or impossible because You want Your son/ daughter free.*

As Love does this, say out loud: "As an act of my will, I choose to let _____ off the hook for _____." (Then let all the offense and ugly rip. It's OK, you need to get it out of you!)

List all the ugly here:

_____

_____

_____

_____

(If you need more space, get your journal.) Do this for each person/group that comes up. If you are triggered or need more help, do not hesitate to seek it. I am trusting Love to guide you and help you! There is freedom on the other side of this!

After you are done with all that, congratulations, the yucky but crucial part is over!

Pappa, now reveal to Your son/daughter Who You really are, how You really feel about what happened, where You were, and what You were doing. If You need to take them out of dangerous places, I trust You will. Minister to areas of harm, pain, danger, disappointment, grief, loss, anger...What do You want Your son/daughter to know?

Let Love speak in those words, thoughts, pictures, feelings, impressions, knowings, or other manifestations to minister to all those places that really need Him. TAKE YOUR TIME!!!! Write down what you are getting. If you need more space, use your journal.

Love is showing me:

_____

_____

_____

Happy Flavors

The word of God says that He does not change:

> Jesus Christ is the same yesterday and today and forever. (Hebrews 13:8 NIV)

> My dearly loved brothers and sisters, don't be misled. Every good gift bestowed, every perfect gift received comes to us from above, courtesy of the Father of lights. He is consistent. He won't change His mind or play tricks in the shadows. We have a special role in His plan. He calls us to life by His message of truth so that we will show the rest of his creatures His goodness and love. (James 1:16-18 Voice)

God also doesn't start out tasting like tutti-frutti and end up tasting like stinky socks. His idea is to surprise you not with a bad aftertaste, but with His goodness above all you could think or even hope for (Ephesians 3:20 AMP):

> Now to Him Who is able to [carry out His purpose and] do super-abundantly more than all that we dare ask or think [infinitely beyond our greatest prayers, hopes, or dreams], according to His power that is at work within us.

I remember when I was talking about what it means to become a believer with my highly intelligent, liberal, skeptical, but fabulous mother. She kept on looking for the catch. Her response was something to the extent of, "Jesus sounds good, but, whoa, once you get hooked in – what are you in for? What's the catch?"

These are very good questions. Questions like that never offend or throw God off one moment. They may throw off man's evangelistic programs, but God has a different idea of evangelism. It is His goodness (that does not change for one moment) that draws all men to change their minds and agree with Him (Romans 2:4 NIV):

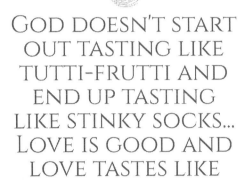

GOD DOESN'T START OUT TASTING LIKE TUTTI-FRUTTI AND END UP TASTING LIKE STINKY SOCKS... LOVE IS GOOD AND LOVE TASTES LIKE GOOD.

Or do you show contempt for the riches of his kindness, forbearance, and patience, not realizing that God's kindness is intended to lead you to repentance?

Love is good and Love "tastes like good." However, we have seen so much of life that is not like that, we constantly seem to be waiting for the barf flavor to show up.

But I have one word for you: relax. Love is good – totally good. Always good. Unchangingly good. Fascinatingly, intoxicatingly good. God and His Kingdom are never boring. And He is totally for you, right here, right now.

Love has many flavors, but all of them delightful and satisfying! My fervent prayer is that you grow in your connection with Love.

Let Him reveal His goodness to you and allow Him to define what flavor(s) of goodness look like for you right where you are at. Ask Him to reveal Himself, and be patient with yourself and with the pace you are connecting with Him. He is ever so patient with you and will help you do so.

Pink spoons, anyone?

3.
WHO AM I?

Who Am I?

How many times have you tried to figure yourself out? Who am I?

Humanity is in an identity crisis. It is a silent battle that expresses itself in a myriad of very loud ways. When you don't know who you are, you are adrift. When you have misidentified yourself, you are in a battle to fit into a "you" that never seems to and never will fit. Because of this, many people spend their whole lives throwing themselves into one career, role, religious system, passion, hobby, fashion statement, musical genre, you-name-it, after the next. They can't settle down or rest because the promise of peace and of "finding ourselves" never materializes. And they are on to the next mirage, promising fulfillment, but always just out of reach. How tragic!

Society, peers, culture, coworkers, parents, religion, popular culture, sports, music, the fashion industry, politics, and an endless variety of other voices have lots to say about who they think you are. Or it is more like who they think you should be or shouldn't be. Then there are all the roles we play and the hats we wear. There are the things we like and the things we dislike.

All these voices can be very loud and conflicting, and they are often nonstop. No wonder we can't rest. No wonder we are confused! We have all been there in the midst of that tug of war. And, if we slow down and quiet down enough, the nagging question remains, "Who am I *really*?"

God has a lot to say about who you are. It is clear, you are on his mind. The word of God says:

> *How precious it is, Lord, to realize that you are thinking about me constantly! I can't even count how many times a day your thoughts turn toward me. And when I waken in the morning, you are still thinking of me! (Psalm 139:17-18 TLB)*

His Word says that His thoughts about you are as many as the sands of the earth (Psalm 139:17-18 KJV). Think about all the beaches of the world. And then think about those shores going deep into the oceans of the world and the thickness of the bottom sands of the seas. Think about the sands in the deserts. Think about the sands in the mountains and in the main lands. Each grain is a thought about you. And His thoughts about you outnumber those.

It is clear God is obsessed, in the best sense of the word, with His creation, and He, make no mistake, He is obsessed with YOU!

LOVE IS OBSESSED, IN THE BEST SENSE OF THE WORD, WITH HIS CREATION, AND HE, MAKE NO MISTAKE, HE IS OBSESSED WITH YOU!

As the Creator, God crafted you with unique strokes and delighted in you before you even knew you were a "you." His word says,

For You formed my innermost parts; You knit me [together] in my mother's womb. I will give thanks and praise to You, for I am fearfully and wonderfully made; Wonderful are Your works, and my soul knows it very well. My frame was not hidden from You, when I was being formed in secret, and intricately and skillfully formed [as if embroidered with many colors] in the depths of the earth. Your eyes have seen my unformed substance; and in Your book were all written the days that were appointed for me, when as yet there was not one of them [even taking shape]. (Psalm 139:13-16 AMP)

The Voice version of the Bible puts it like this:

For You shaped me, inside and out. You knitted me together in my mother's womb long before I took my first breath. I will offer You my grateful heart, for I am Your unique creation, filled with wonder and awe. You have approached even the smallest details with excellence; Your works are wonderful; I carry this knowledge deep within my soul. You see all things; nothing about me was hidden from You as I took shape in secret, carefully crafted in the heart of the earth before I was born from its womb. You see all things; You saw me growing, changing in my mother's womb; every detail of my life was already written in Your book; You established the length of my life before I ever tasted the sweetness of it.

God was so precise and enamored with you that He wrote a book about you to document each detail of your life. He knit and crafted you in your mother's womb.

The word of God says that you are His workmanship (Ephesians 2:10) created to do good works which He planned beforehand and made ready for you to do before the foundation of the world.

The Amplified Version says,

For we are His workmanship [His own master work, a work of art], created in Christ Jesus [reborn from above spiritually transformed, renewed, ready to be used] for good works, which God prepared [for us] beforehand [taking paths which He set], so that we would walk in them [living the good life which He prearranged and made ready for us].

Interestingly, the word "workmanship" is the Greek word *poiēma* where we get, you guessed it, the word "poem." You are God's poem!

Poiēma can be translated as follows:
1. a product, such as a fabric, literally or figuratively
2. a thing that is made
3. workmanship

You are literally cut out of the same bolt of fabric as your Creator. Hey you, "get down" with your bad self!

YOU ARE LITERALLY CUT OUT OF THE SAME BOLT OF FABRIC AS YOUR CREATOR.

Contrary to many of our deepest suspicions and fears, God made no rejects, throwbacks, throwaways, misfits, outcasts, or do-overs. He was not confused, distracted, disinterested, cheap, or underhanded when He crafted you. He is not some cruel cosmic jokester. He has no identity crisis. He is Love, and Love does not change (Hebrews 13:8). He is the daddy you always wanted but never knew you could have – or better said, was already yours. And He is wild about you. You are preapproved by Love (Ephesians 1:3-6). And Love has excellent taste. He never cuts corners.

Apparently there is something about who you intrinsically are that has captured God's heart and mind. He is justly obsessed!

But in order for you to know the real you, you have to know the One Who created you.

Your You-ness

What makes up identity? When we run into that rare authentic person, who knows who they are and who actually *likes* who they are, whether or not others like them (what a thought), it is so refreshing! We are drawn to them even if we do not know why. Even if we do not like their politics or lifestyle or we can't really relate to them, there is something about them that draws us. The word of God says that when a person's ways please the Lord, He makes even his enemies to be at peace

THERE IS SOMETHING ABOUT WHO YOU INTRINSICALLY ARE THAT HAS CAPTURED GOD'S HEART AND MIND.

with him (Proverbs 16:7). What could be more pleasing to the Lord than when we manifest ourselves as sons and daughters to the specifications that He made before the foundation of the world?

This sheds a whole new light on "this is My beloved son in whom I am well-pleased" (Matthew 3:17; 17:5, 2 Peter 1:17). Being in Christ as a son or daughter automatically makes *you* the one with whom He is well pleased. There is nothing to separate you from your heavenly Father Who is simply wild about you!

Jesus went first as the Father's firstborn so that you could be among His many brothers and sisters, co-reigning and co-heirs with Him (Romans 5:17; 8:14-17, 29; Revelation 5:10). He died on the cross so that you could be grafted in Him and Him in you as one with

Him and hence, one with the Trinity (Romans 6:4-10; 11:17; Galatians 2:20; Colossians 1:27).

And He did this all before the foundation of the world (Revelation 13:8)! Yeah, my mind is boggling too! But there it is in black and white. But this black and white is not just any words, it represents Christ as *the* Word. And, because He is the Creator of all good things, He gets to have the last word, independent of our feelings, experiences, or personal opinions about it. And this word is Truth. And the beauty of Truth is that He sets you free. He sets you free to be you.

And He wants you to manifest the real you – the authentic you. This version of you is so attractive that it draws people to you and to the Christ in you, the Source of the glory you intrinsically carry. Yes, we are drawn to the authentic.

LOVE SETS YOU FREE TO BE YOU.

We may not be able to pinpoint it with our natural senses and understanding, but like Coke Classic, we know it when we've hit "the real thing."

Merriam-Webster Dictionary defines identity as the "distinguishing character or personality of an individual."

The truth is that you are distinctly "you," even if you don't have a clue yet how fabulous that actually is.

Your "you-ness" has already been established! It is not something you put on, paint on, Photoshop, put in an updo, or perfect an act for. It is a process of unveiling and discovery. As you discover the One, Who created you, you can encounter who Love really made you to be. Let's unpack our relationship with Love a little deeper.

In Love, Love in Us, One with Love

You were established before the foundation of the world. Let's dive in a little to this deep but yummy mystery!

Scripture says that Jesus was the Lamb slain before the foundation of the world (Revelation 13:8).

Weirder than that, the word of God says that you were mystically crucified with Him (Galatians 2:20; Romans 6:3-6).

Dang! Here is a passage to ponder:

> *I have been crucified with Christ and I no longer live, but Christ lives in me. The life I now live in the body, I*

AS YOU DISCOVER THE ONE, WHO CREATED YOU, YOU CAN ENCOUNTER WHO LOVE REALLY MADE YOU TO BE.

live by faith in the Son of God, who loved me and gave himself for me. (Galatians 2:20 NIV)

And again:

Or don't you know that all of us who were baptized into Christ Jesus were baptized into his death? We were therefore buried with him through baptism into death in order that, just as Christ was raised from the dead through the glory of the Father, we too may live a new life. For if we have been united with him in a death like his, we will certainly also be united with him in a resurrection like his. For we know that our old self was crucified with him so that the body ruled by sin might be done away with, that we should no longer be slaves to sin. (Romans 6:3-6, 10 NIV)

So when Christ died on the cross, somehow mystically you, with your old sinful nature, died with Him and rose again with Him when He rose again. And you rose as a new creation never seen before:

For Christ's love compels us, because we are convinced that one died for all, and therefore all died. And he died for all that those who live should no longer live for themselves but for him who died for them and was raised again. Therefore if any man be in Christ, he is a new creature: old things are passed away; behold, all things are become new. (2 Corinthians 5:14-15, 17 NIV)

The word of God also brings out our union or oneness with Christ because of what He accomplished on the cross:

But whoever is united with the Lord is one with him in spirit. (1 Corinthians 6:17 NIV)

Therefore, if anyone is united with the Anointed One, that person is a new creation. The old life is gone – and see – a new life has begun! (2 Corinthians 5:17 Voice)

With that, Christ is "in the believer" (Colossians 1:27).

To them God has chosen to make known among the Gentiles the glorious riches of this mystery, which is Christ in you, the hope of glory. (Colossians 1:27 NIV)

And the believer is "in Christ":

For you died, and your life is now hidden with Christ in God. When Christ, Who is your life, appears, then you also will appear with Him in glory. (Colossians 3:3-4 NIV)

So in Christ Jesus you are all children of God through faith, for all of you who were baptized into Christ have clothed yourselves with Christ. (Galatians 3:26 NIV)

So what does all this mean? It means that you as a believer died with Christ, rose with Christ, were placed in Christ, Christ was placed in you, and you are one with Him. And this all was accomplished before you were ever born.

Because God is Love, this means that you as a believer are in Love, Love is in you, and you are one with Love and all that happened before you ever knew you wanted or needed Love – before the foundation of the world.

All this is also available as a tangible reality to everyone who does *not* consider themselves to be a believer, because Christ or Love died for the sins of the *entire world.* I like the Message version for this:

YOU ARE IN LOVE, LOVE IS IN YOU, AND YOU ARE ONE WITH LOVE AND ALL THAT HAPPENED BEFORE YOU EVER KNEW YOU WANTED OR NEEDED LOVE BEFORE THE FOUNDATION OF THE WORLD.

I write this, dear children, to guide you out of sin. But if anyone does sin, we have a Priest-Friend in the presence of the Father: Jesus Christ, righteous Jesus. When he served as a sacrifice for our sins, he solved the sin problem for good not only ours, but the whole world's. (1 John 2:1-3 MSG)

What all that means is that you were a distinct "you" before the world was ever created!

God did not create you as a blob. He did not botch His work or get started and lose interest or forget to finish you. No, He had a distinct "you" in mind and, therefore, He is the One and only One who is qualified, primed, and, frankly, stoked to reveal you to you! He wants you to know who you are more than you want to get to know yourself! He is your one and only truly qualified Source. Love created you and knows you from the inside out!!

And don't be scared that you'll be disappointed when you finally discover yourself or that you will be what you always feared. You will love the real you, because you were created in Love, by Love Himself!

Answering The Yeah-Buts

I can hear the "yeah-buts" or "you don't knows". People are afraid that they are not enough or that they are too much. The fear is, "if only people really knew me" – Love does! Every "yeah-but" is silenced, quieted, comforted, healed, and restored by Love. So yeah, Love is not only a really big deal, but He also embodies and saturates the whole deal and sweeps you right up along with it.

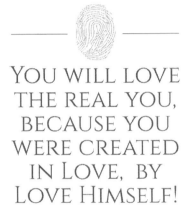

YOU WILL LOVE THE REAL YOU, BECAUSE YOU WERE CREATED IN LOVE, BY LOVE HIMSELF!

When Love defines "you" to you, that definition will be lovely. You are lookin' really good, even if you do not know it yet. So you might have to settle down and start loving yourself. Give it up already. God doesn't want a truce. He wants to exchange all He is for all you are. And He is so smitten with you that He is not suspicious that He got the raw end of the deal. He already put all of Himself on the table. The question is whether or not you are going to trade up.

Our poets may be counting all the ways to love. But God never felt the need to quantify the unquantifiable. He just laughs in His delight – He simply cannot get enough of you. Trying to quantify His love would be absurd. How much time do you have? It's a good thing He made you for eternity – you'll need it to experience all that Love!

Our hearts are complex things. We were made for love, but the pain of rejection and tragedy and lovelessness and, you know, the stuff you've gone through, causes us all to, at various points, harden and protect our hearts. Sometimes our hearts die. Sometimes they turn to stone. But God...He is the One Who never fails. He is the master cardiothoracic surgeon. He is the supernatural electric shock to jumpstart an arrested heart. He will even gladly transplant His heart into yours, if you need it. He is not hard up for workable parts.

LOVE JUST LAUGHS IN HIS DELIGHT – HE SIMPLY CANNOT GET ENOUGH OF YOU.

And they are not secondhand retreads. God is very picky about what He provides for His kids. He might be considered the obnoxious parent in the room, except for the fact that everyone gets to be His favorite, if they'll just wake up to that very juicy, very real fact.

And the Bottom Line Is

So what does this all mean in the anatomy of your identity? It's simply and vastly this: You have to know the One Who created you before you can know yourself. You look just like Him. And did I mention He's gorgeous? So quit messing with your hair or lack of it, and settle down. Love is beautiful, and it looks amazing on you. But it also looks unique to you. God didn't break the mold because He was worried some other defectives would make it through. He revels in uniqueness and joyfully loves to celebrate the you-ness of you.

LOVE IS BEAUTIFUL, AND IT LOOKS AMAZING ON YOU!

Getting to know yourself means getting to know the One Who loved you and gave Himself up for you (Galatians 2:20). And in giving Himself up for you, Love really doesn't think He got the short end of the stick. God is a wise investor, and He chose to invest in you – heavily (Ephesians 1:3-6). He's all in and holding nothing back. He's given us all things richly to enjoy – starting with Himself first (1 Timothy 6:17).

So apparently, despite what neglectful, abusive, or even maniacal people have said or done, your value has irrevocably been decided. You are incalculably invaluable. And this was decided before you even had the chance to do anything brilliant. If Jesus was slain before the foundation of the world, the price to purchase you back – your value – does not stem from anything that you could ever do or not do. This is great news to the flops, failures, rejects, and outcasts. This is ever so insulting to those who have based their value on what they do or how they look or how much is in their bank account.

But, in the same breath, let's be clear. You were born to be brilliant in your own way and in your own sphere of influence. But that brilliance is a reflection of your intrinsic worth, not the source of it. He is the Source of all your brilliance, so you can't take credit for

YOU WERE BORN TO BE BRILLIANT IN YOUR OWN WAY AND IN YOUR OWN SPHERE OF INFLUENCE.

it (Colossians 1:27; Ephesians 2:8-10). You are brilliant because you are so valuable, and thus, you are free to be naturally supernaturally brilliant.

Stated in another way: You are not valuable based on your brilliance. You are valuable based on *His* brilliance. And that never changes (Hebrews 13:8) – productive or not; beautiful or homely; wealthy or debt-ridden; righteous acting or sin-ridden; genius or idiot.

20/20

Only Love has 20/20 vision. Only Loves sees the way things were originally intended and calls people up to the truth of how they were originally designed. There is no condemnation in Christ Jesus (Romans 8:1). The world may condemn you, but Love convicts you of who you truly are (John 16:8). You were created in Love. Anything other than love is going against the grain of your design.

ONLY GOD, ONLY LOVE, GETS TO DEFINE US. ANYTHING ELSE IS A MERE SHADOW AT BEST AND AN OUTRIGHT LIE AT WORST.

We have gotten so enamored with the power of sin to define and limit us, that we have missed our redemption from it. Sin, in ourselves and others, does not get to define us. For that matter, success and good works do not define us. Only God – only Love – gets to define us. Anything else is a mere shadow at best and an outright lie at worst.

We have gotten so taken in by our performance, stellar, miserable, or indifferent, that we have forgotten that we were called to "be" first, and do out of our "being." We are human "beings" not human "doings." We were called to be human beings created in the image and likeness of Love, to do things that reflect that image. You were created to be amazing and "do amazing" out of that way of being. But until we get the "being," we will always strive in the doing. Ask me how I know. We will talk more about being delivered from the trap of performance later, so stay tuned in.

Daddy Warbucks

God is masterful at what He does. He chases down the orphan to reveal that they never were an orphan. Pappa God is the Daddy Warbucks of all Daddy Warbucks – remember the musical Orphan Annie? You are no Orphan Annie. You need to stop confessing yours is a "hard knock life." The sun is not waiting to "come out tomorrow." The Son already came. You're already home. If you don't know it yet, it is time to let Pappa renew your mind. It's way past time to settle down and let Pappa luxuriate His love all over you. He's a doting Daddy. And you get to be His beloved child, no matter what your age. And you can trust Him to help you "get it!" Holy Spirit is not called the Teacher, leading and guiding you into all Truth, for nothing (John 16:13, the Amplified is the most helpful one here). You get to be His favorite. Just ask Him. He'll be thrilled to tell you! Don't ask me how we can all be His favorites, but it is true. This is a happy mystery that God is all about and all over.

United with Love

The anatomy of your identity is wrapped up and inseparable from your position as one with Love. Love was compelled to the cross out of love. And the finished work of that cross does not need finishing. It doesn't need touch-ups or polishing. God really never needed our help. And, as insulting as it may be and counter to our deeply in-grained "doing" programming, He *still* does not need our help. He accomplished saving you and scooping up humanity all by His very big not-so-lonesome self (1 John 2:2). He gets all the credit! He just asks us to believe (John 6:29). And then He helps us with our unbelief (Mark 9:24). Because, let's face it, we tend to be dense. And He lovingly helps us with our denseness. He understands that apart from Him, we can do not one little thing of eternal value (John 15:5).

> LOVE IS THE ALPHA AND OMEGA, AND HE SWOOPS US UP INTO EVERY LETTER OF HIS BEING AND INVITES US TO PARTICIPATE IN THE DANCE OF HIS DIVINITY.

We need a revelation of what it all encompasses right here, right now for us and for all of humanity, right where we are at. And He is the One to enlighten the eyes of our under-standing so we may know what is the hope He has called us to, the riches hidden inside us, and His mighty power available to us who believe (Ephesians 1:17-21). He is the One to get us there from here. He is the author and the finisher of our faith. So we can put the heavy lifting on Him (Hebrews 12:2).

And even though He is the alpha and omega, He swoops us up into every letter of His being and invites us to participate in the dance of His divinity. And while our minds boggle, He happily goes about demolishing every bit of us that thinks we ever could or ever need to earn it.

Intimacy Blockers

God's fervent, sweet, and passionate desire is for intimacy with His kids, His friends, and His bride – all of which you were made to be through Love's sacrifice.

Intimacy can be a scary, if not a terrifying thing, when there has been pain or abuse in this area. But let's be clear: You were made for intimacy! It is such a place of life and power that withholding, destroying, or perverting it has been a priority objective of the enemy of our souls. And that means that precious few, if any, have been left unscathed.

WITH RESPECT TO GOD, SIN HAS BEEN FORGIVEN – PERIOD! AND HE DIDN'T POLL THE HUMAN RACE WITH HOW THEY FEEL ABOUT IT.

Many people really struggle with connecting to God intimately. Very frequently this is because they feel unworthy and too ashamed to get close. Sometimes

God is flat out a terrifying reflection in people's minds of the abuse they experienced at the hands of people who were supposed to represent Love, but represented the devil. This is all too diabolical when that picture was implanted as a representation of God. No wonder people struggle!

But yay, there is huge sweeping hope wherever you are at! You don't have to been denied, and you should insist that you *won't* be denied! Rebellion is a good and righteous thing when you rebel against the enemy of your soul and his diabolical plans to destroy your life, the lives of your loved ones, and generations to follow you! Understand rebellion should not be against people, but against the one who has moved through people, and how that has manifested in people. Ultimately, people are not our enemies, and we are barking up the wrong tree if that is where we are wasting our energy. You don't have to and shouldn't cuddle up to a serial killer. But understand there is no one who was born evil to be evil. satan (and I use a small "s" to remind him and all of us that he is a small "s" next to a big "G" God) and his minions are the problem. he is liar, deceiver, thief, destroyer, and serial killer, who preys upon the innocent and vulnerable. He wants to manipulate people to be an instrument of the very evil that was thrust upon them.

Often because of what has happened, people do the only things they know to do to medicate pain. Because love was violated in their lives, they violate love in some way against God, against themselves, or against others. There's a word for that and it is not popular or PC, but it is called sin. And sin is sin, and God makes no bones about it and has no favorites in this department. He never pretends sin is not sin, and He doesn't look at it with the moral relativism that people like to. It is a level playing ground. But with that, as I said before, with respect to Him, sin has been forgiven – period! And He didn't poll the human race with how they feel about it. But just because it may be forgiven, God is also passionate about getting you out of agreement with it because it is killing, stealing, and destroying you and others around you. In sin – He does not condemn you. He has condemned the very sin principle itself.

I want to unpack this very briefly for you. Romans 5:17 (AMP) says:

SELF-RIGHTEOUSNESS STINKS BECAUSE IT CAUSES YOU TO LOOK TO YOURSELF RATHER THAN LOVE.

For if because of one man's trespass (lapse, offense) death reigned through that one, much more surely will those who receive [God's] overflowing grace (unmerited favor) and the free gift of righteousness [putting them into right standing with Himself] reign as kings in life through the one Man Jesus Christ (the Messiah, the Anointed One).

That means that, because of Adam's sin and the subsequent fall of humankind, death was released where there was no death previously. But for those who receive what Jesus did for them (and He will definitely help you do this everywhere the breakdown is), God freely gives them a righteous, no-shame, no-condemnation standing with Him. This standing no one can never earn, pay back, or steal from others.

When you try to earn it or pay God back for it, regardless of how good your intentions may be, it is called self-righteousness. And though God has forgiven it, self-righteousness stinks because it causes you to look to yourself rather than Him. You have just functionally disconnected yourself from His grace.

BECAUSE YOU ARE MARKED WITH HIS RIGHTEOUSNESS, LOVE WILL CALL YOU TO OWN YOUR STUFF AND CLEAN UP YOUR MESS AS BEST YOU CAN.

Love's objective is that you just freely enjoy your righteous standing regardless of the junk that you did and do. It was not fair that you were born into the consequences of Adam's sin and what that meant for your family line. So Love, never to be outdone, overcome, or impressed by the "power" of evil, took it upon Himself. He took care of how sin tried to separate you from Him, define you, control you, mock you, degrade you, torment you, harm others through you, and spit you out.

He will call you up to that true, lovely, righteous nature of how He created you to be. In a very real sense, Love has marked you with His righteousness. Because you are marked with His righteousness, He will call you to own your stuff and clean up your mess as best you can. But He will not condemn you that you are not there yet. And you will not get there until you start and fight the fight to continue to identify with who you are through His eyes: righteous, holy, blameless, and lovely. And because you are forgiven, He is calling you to forgive yourself even as you own your mess.

Hang with me for two more verses. This is super important.

> *For what the Law could not do [that is, overcome sin and remove its penalty, its power] being weakened by the flesh [man's nature without the Holy Spirit], God did: He sent His own Son in the likeness of sinful man as an offering for sin. And He condemned sin in the flesh [subdued it and overcame it in the person of His own Son]. (Romans 8:3 AMP)*

So the Law, which is the rules and regulations that are designed to stem sin, has no power to cause that to happen. The word of God says it actually strengthens and empowers sin (1 Corinthians 15:56). You can see this by the futility of New Year's resolutions. My husband regularly goes to the YMCA. Every year he is amazed how the swimming lanes and workout machines get ridiculously crowded the first week of January. But by February, there is no more congestion. It is actually rather dead. What happened? Beating themselves with the "I-am-going-to" and "not-going-to" resolutions does not empower people to do or not to do. So they feel discouraged, condemned, and disempowered, and the pounds and flabbiness pack on. So with this and in every other area we have struggled and continue to struggle with sin, we need help. Enter Jesus before the foundation of the world and then two thousand-ish years ago on the cross.

Love condemned sin as an entity itself in His fleshly body (Romans 8:3). Sin as an entity and not just behavior is the Greek word *hamartia*, which means "to miss the mark" or "err." Love condemned sin because sin harms His beloved creation. Love does not condemn you even when you are foolish enough to partner with sin and partner with it big time:

> *Therefore there is now no condemnation [no guilty verdict, no punishment] for those who are in Christ Jesus [who believe in Him as personal Lord and Savior]. (Romans 8:1 AMP)*

WHEN YOU, THROUGH LOVE'S EMPOWERMENT (GRACE) START AND STICK WITH SEEING YOURSELF AS PURE, RIGHTEOUS, BLAMELESS, HOLY, AND POWERFUL, YOU CAN SHAKE OFF SIN LIKE A STINKY FILTHY COAT THAT DOESN'T FIT ANYMORE.

Outside of Christ, there is plenty of condemnation – not from God, but from the devil and his minions and from you in and of yourself. Is sin okay? Absolutely not! Are you okay, even if you are diving into it, bathing in it, and eating it for breakfast and serving it up to the masses? Unequivocally, irrevocably, yes! And because of that, yes, you absolutely can, and of course you absolutely should, shake that mess off your fabulous righteous self. When you, through Love's empowerment (grace) start and stick with seeing yourself as pure, righteous, blameless, holy, and powerful, you can shake off sin like a stinky filthy coat that doesn't fit anymore. Sin doesn't fit because you are seeing yourself more and more rightly. You should clean up your mess as best you can – because God made you in Love to love. He made you honorable, even if you have not scored highly in the honor department, because He is honorable. He will empower you on all fronts.

YOU ARE WORTH WHATEVER IT TAKES TO GET FREE AND BE RESTORED AND RECOMPENSED!

Now for some of you, the issue holding you back from intimacy with God is not your own sin, but the sin that was forced upon you with physical, emotional, sexual, or spiritual abuse. Often the victim takes the blame on as theirs and with that wears a cloak of shame they can't seem to shake. That shame and powerlessness colors and mars the very fabric of how they see or perhaps have always seen themselves. If this is you, you will need healing, perhaps massive healing. That will come through encountering Love and His Truth.

Perhaps you blame God for "not being there" or "letting it happen." You will have to forgive Him in order to receive healing from Him. I am not saying that God sinned, but in your heart of hearts, it may really *feel* that way! If you are ticked off at God, you will not allow yourself to receive from Him or allow Him to give you what He wants to give you. Forgiving Him is the starting point here for you to see Him rightly, see where He was and what He was doing to get the healing and answers you need. You will find He is not mad that you are angry or enraged at Him. But He does want you to get past that so you can heal.

You are worth whatever time and expense it takes for this! Love never was or will be your abuser. Love was and will be your rescuer and deliverer. I have seen it over and over and over. With all the people and their horror stories that I have ministered to, I have never seen God *not* come through, if people will stick with it. You are worth whatever it takes to get free and be restored and recompensed! And you never need apologize for it taking the time it may take. You are running your own race!

Love Encounter Break #3

We have delved into the reality of our oneness with Love. He is inside you, and you are inside Him. This is a concept that is often given a nod, but not often experienced to much of an extent by the very people Love is one with. Many people long for that experience but have been frustrated by a lack of satisfying experience. I have heard it again and again. Those of you who have not longed for experiencing Love, might I suggest that you are not connecting with your own heart? You were *made* for this, so why are you settling? God longs for that experience as well – on a regular basis! Love wants you to experience Him! He's safe, He's Life. He's healing. Love is also really fun and not straight-laced or constipated at all! If you think or even suspect that God is a killjoy, might I remind you that Jesus, the express image of the Father (Hebrews 1:3), did His first miracle at a party, turning water into wine (John 2:1-11). He rebuked a rebellious prophet through the mouth of a donkey (Numbers 22:28). When Elijah challenged the prophets of Baal, a false god, to a showdown, he taunted them by saying maybe their god was napping or out relieving himself. God did not bleep any of that out, even if some translators did (1 Kings 18:26-28). He is so fun that joy is one-third of the kingdom of heaven – righteousness, peace, and joy (Romans 14:17)! So relax and have fun as you open yourself up to oneness with Love, you in Him and Him in you!

Let me pray this over you. Just receive.

Pappa, I thank You that You are a God Who wants to enjoy Your kids and Who wants them to experience and enjoy You! I thank You that You are safe and good and healing and fun! I thank You that it was Your idea and Your heart to bring Your sons and daughters close and help them to experience intimacy with You. I ask You to help Your children experience for themselves what intimacy, oneness, You in them and them in You, is like. And I thank You that You are well able and stoked to help Your kids with this wherever they need it! I thank You for making this safe for those who may struggle with feeling safe.

I thank You for making this powerful for those who are flatlined or lukewarm in this. I thank You for making this fun for those who have felt so much heavy toil. I thank You for being whatever dimension of Yourself Your kids need!

In the name and through the blood of Jesus Christ I forbid any hindrances, harassment, and assignments or any masquerading by spirits who were not born in the flesh of a virgin, who did not die for the sins of the entire world on the cross, who were not raised on the third day and seated at the right hand of the Father.

I thank You, Holy Spirit, for leading each and every person into the Truth of Who You, Jesus, and Father God are as Love.

I thank You, Pappa, for heaven invading earth right here, right now, right where each and every person is at. I thank You for fabulous life-giving encounters and helping each and every person enter in to those encounters!

Now let yourself relax and let Love speak in those words, thoughts, pictures, feelings, impressions, knowings, or other manifestations of

His oneness with you, Him in you and you in Him. Jot down anything you are getting, however small, even if you are not sure it is God. You can review this later or bring it to a trusted spiritual leader to help you judge it.

Relax. Let God do the heavy lifting. Let Him surprise you. Be patient with yourself if this is new. He will help you! You will get better and better at this as you practice! If at any time this really does not feel safe to do, shut it down, and you can go back later when you are in a better place. But if Love is asking you to push through your fears so He can minister to them, heed that. If you need more space, grab or make a new journal.

My encounter with Love – one with Him, Him in me and me in Him:

_____

_____

_____

_____

If you are having trouble, ask God if you need to forgive Him (i.e., for not seeming to be there when you needed Him, for not seeming to back you up, for you being born into an unhealthy or abusive family, for a tragedy, for...). Keep in mind you may not feel angry, but the issue is not anger, it is an offense that is still there whether or not you still feel anger. If you feel you have already forgiven and He is leading you to do this again, trust Him that He knows what He is doing. If you are sensing this, start by saying, "As an act of my will, I choose to forgive you God for..." (And let her rip in full technicolor. It is safe and healthy for you to get it out of you.)

If others come up in your mind to forgive, do the same with them until you feel the forgiveness issue is released for this time.

Then let me pray:

> *Pappa, I thank You for revealing all of the offense in people's hearts and helping them to get it out of them! So in this place, what do You want to show them now?*

If you are still not connecting to God, ask Him, "What lie am I believing about You or connecting with You that is hindering this?" Jot down what you are getting:

_____

_____

_____

_____

_____

Let me pray:

Pappa, what truth do You want to show them about that lie?

Write down what you get. Keep in mind there may be a series of lies that you may need to take the time to let Him deal with, so repeat this as much as necessary.

_____

_____

_____

_____

Once you go through those lies and receive truth(s), let me pray:

Pappa, thank You for helping Your kids! I thank You, Holy Spirit, for leading each and every person into the Truth of Who You, Jesus, and Father God are as Love. I thank You, Pappa, and I ask You again, on behalf of these, for heaven to invade earth right here, right now, right where each and every person is. I thank You for fabulous life-giving encounters of their oneness with You, You in them, and them in You, and helping each and every person enter in to those encounters and keeping them safe!

Write down what you get.

_____

_____

_____

_____

_____

_____

_____

If you are still struggling, you are probably needing some healing and help with this. It is really a mind renewal process to the wholeness you *already have* in Christ, so that you can experience what is already yours. You are coming *from* a place of victory, not scraping to get *to* a place of victory. In your struggle to get this, you are totally not alone. This is quite common, and with help this gets easier and easier, so you can get to be a pro! Know that I am actively standing with you and for you in this and am trusting Love to lead you exactly where you need to go to get the help you need and the help He wants to provide for you! He is *masterful* at this, and I trust Him implicitly with you and for you!

Identity & Identity Fraud

When you are at a store, a bank, an airport, or the Division of Motor Vehicles and you are asked to prove your identity, you pull out an identification card, a driver's license, a passport, or birth certificate. This is something that shows who a person is – a document, card, etc., with your name and other information about you, and often includes your photograph. You are saying, "Yes, this is me, and I can prove it."

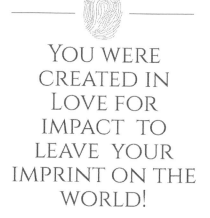

YOU WERE CREATED IN LOVE FOR IMPACT TO LEAVE YOUR IMPRINT ON THE WORLD!

Identity fraud is altogether way too common in the natural realm. And it is a mess to clean up. But I suspect it is even more common and definitely more tragic when your identity is stolen in the spiritual realm. When you don't know who you are, you may live years or even your whole life as someone else. You get cheated from experiencing the real you. And the world gets cheated from experiencing the real you and the impact you were born for.

Every human being was conceived with a unique complement of DNA. This was not some random biochemical happening. Remember, you were intricately knit together in your mother's womb, crafted as a masterpiece to do good works that you were ordained to do before the foundation of the world (Psalm 139:15-16; Ephesians 2:10). You are a poem that was crafted to inspire the world.

The time in the womb is a secret miraculous time. As you were being formed in the womb, the dermis (lower layer of your skin) and epidermis (upper layer of your skin) were also forming. The amniotic fluid swirled around on the pads of your fingertips. This created the pattern of your unique fingerprints that would identify you and your "touch on the world" for your entire life.

You were created in Love for impact – to leave your imprint on the world!

But that is not all. God is so intimately involved not only with the details of you being knit together in your mother's womb, but also with your birth, and your entire life. Remember His book about you? The Voice version puts it this way:

> You see all things; nothing about me was hidden from You as I took shape in secret, carefully crafted in the heart of the earth before I was born from its womb. You see all things; You saw me growing, changing in my mother's womb; Every detail of my life was already written in Your book; You established the length of my life before I ever tasted the sweetness of it. (Psalm 139:15-16)

This was really brought home for me during a time when I was in an overwhelming amount of pain surrounding the details of my conception, development in the womb, and birth. Rejection and abandonment, real or erroneously imprinted, clung to me in a shroud of pain and shame that seemed to define and mark who I was. "What is wrong with me?" had really dogged me since before I was born. More specifics of that and my story are given in Chapter 9.

In seeking the Lord specifically about this, He answered and ministered to me in a vision. He took me to myself in the womb and showed me myself as a frail little embryo. But this embryo was His pride, His joy, and His delight. I was resting on the tip of His finger, and He was showing me off. "Look!!!! Here she is!!!!" There was an eruption in heaven. Yes, I was HIS! My frail tissue sank into the ridges of His fingertip. And His very fingerprint was imprinting itself into my whole body. My total being was being marked as His, in the best, most ecstatic, most joyful, most irreversible way! I was marked as His – chosen and set apart!

There are many ways we can connect to God. In the introduction, I talked about God interacting with His kids through their five spiritual senses, through an internal knowing, through God thoughts, though supernatural signs and wonders, and through angelic visitations. He also speaks to us through natural circumstances. Of course, He always speaks through His word, and all things must line up with rightly divided scripture and the true nature of God as He is revealed in scripture culminating in the revelation of Christ. If they do not, they must be tossed out. This is to protect us from error.

But I wanted to expand just a bit on the concept of getting visions from the Lord, as I refer to them intermittently throughout the book and this may be new to you. First, visions are scriptural, and you find people receiving godly visions throughout scripture (Genesis 15:1; Numbers 12:6; Ezekiel 40:2; Daniel 4:10; Luke 1:22; Acts 2:17; 10:3; 10:17; 18:19; Revelation 1:9). The prophetic spirit operating is primarily visual, but can be combined with any of the other spiritual senses. There are many wonderful resources available regarding visions and the prophetic, and I encourage you to investigate. What I do want you to remember for now is that when you get something from the Lord, visual or otherwise, it is yours and you can revis-

it it by engaging your spiritual senses and going to that same vision at will. Holy Spirit will help you and expand upon it and can even expand with other spiritual senses. You were created a spiritual being living in a physical body seated in heavenly places right now (1 Corinthians 6:17; Ephesians 2:6). So take advantage of that – there is always more!

YOU ARE MARKED TO MAKE YOUR MARK!

I did this very thing, and as I revisited my mother's womb, I saw Pappa attentively and protectively watching over me as He was knitting me together. His Spirit would brood and hover and whirl around playfully and joyfully as He swirled the amniotic fluid around. In doing so, He was creating His masterpieces on my little finger and toe pads – my unique finger and toe prints. I was not only marked by His mark, but I was to make a mark – an imprint of His design on the world.

YOU ARE THE FABRIC OF GOD'S DELIGHT!

And so are you!!! He is no respecter of persons (1 Peter 1:17).

You are marked to make your mark!

This has been and is His joy over each and every person He has ever sent to planet earth.

This was His joy for you!!!! You were imprinted! And you were destined to imprint a lost and dying world, son/daughter of God!!!

Simple & Simply Adored

It is a simple but profound truth. You have nothing to prove. You have been picked out and crafted as a beautiful masterpiece. You can be you – simply a beloved and doted-on child of God! You can be simple and simply adored!

The Lord said to me recently, "You are the fabric of My delight!" Remember, some of the nuances of *poiēma* in Ephesians 2:10 are "poem" and "fabric"! This means you as well! *You* are the fabric of God's delight!

And from that place, we simply cannot help but manifest brilliance and exploits past our wildest imaginations. He didn't just save you for heaven, but intended for you to manifest the brilliance of heaven inside you. You, as a son or daughter, have inside access. You have already been placed in Christ. You are already seated in heavenly places (Ephesians 2:6). The riches of His inheritance are yours by right of a birth that you frankly had nothing to do with (Ephesians 1:3-6; Romans 8:15-17). This is a killer for that religious part of ourselves that constantly wants to *do something* and to receive credit for something. But the unbelievably good news is that if you weren't responsible for it, you can't mess it up. It is finished, because it really was finished by the One Who is the final Word.

DEPENDENCY AS A SON OR DAUGHTER IS A WONDERFUL THING WHEN YOU HAVE AN AMAZING, OH-SO-CAPABLE AND OH-SO-GOOD DADDY, WHO DOESN'T CHANGE AND DOESN'T CHANGE HIS MIND ABOUT YOU!

As a matter a fact, as a believer, you are not in covenant with God. Hang with me! This is really good news, because we humans, in our own strength, up to our own devices, have shown that we screw things up over and over. Just read pretty much everything from Exodus to

Malachi to get that picture ingrained in your mind. God the Father is in covenant with God the Son (2 Corinthians 5:18-19) and as a believer, you are smack dab in the middle of Him, and He is in the core of you. You can't screw this up. But you also can't boast about your contribution – your faith saving you. It is *His* faith – He is the author and finisher of it (Hebrews 12:2).1 He did ALL the heavy lifting! It truly is finished! Whew! And the church said, "Thanks and amen!"

Our job, should we choose to accept it, is to renew our minds to get into agreement with what God is saying in every area of our being. And we need help to do so. We are utterly dependent on God to get there from here.

Dependency as a son or daughter is a wonderful thing when you have an amazing, oh-so-capable and oh-so-good Daddy, Who doesn't change and doesn't change His mind about you. Even His gifts and callings are without repentance (Romans 11:29). He doesn't take those back if we misbehave or even flat out rebel.

We don't need to drive. We don't need to help God with directions. We don't need to keep one eye open to make sure He doesn't take the wrong exit or run out of gas. We can close our eyes in the backseat and snooze in blissful peace knowing that we are safe and secure and at home, because we are in Him.

So Who Am I?

"Who am I?" starts and ends and is everywhere in between the place of being safe, forgiven, made righteous, and simply adored in Him. We are one with Him through His completed effort that is completely independent of our own efforts. We never outgrow the Gospel. We never become so sophisticated that we can thank God and take it from here. If we are foolish enough to do that, we end up crashing and burning and sooner or later have to run home to Pappa, with our bloodied and banged up selves – and probably have a big mess to clean up. And when we do, He won't tell us, "I told you so," and, "It serves you right." He'll be

YOU ARE CLEAN, BELOVED. YOU ARE RIGHTEOUS. AND YOU ARE WILDLY LOVED.

thrilled we turned to Him. He'll clean up our wounds, help us clean up our mess, set us on the right path, AND redeem the time. Wow!

Those who have been forgiven much, love much (Luke 7:47). But who hasn't been forgiven much? If you don't think that applies to you, you need to examine that Pharisaical self-righteous blindness and check it at the door. Yes, even you are forgiven right along with the rest of those wallowing in different flavors of sin.

Let's be clear. Sin is violating love – toward God, toward yourself, and toward others. We've all been there; it is a level playing ground. That is why Jesus died for the sins of the entire world (1 John 2:2). The *entire world*, including you and me, needed it!

And on the basis of that forgiveness, we can forgive ourselves, clean up our mess, and step into the righteousness that He has made us (2 Corinthians 5:21). In keeping, we must resist condemnation at all points, because condemnation for the believer is illegal in the kingdom (Romans 8:1). He needs you free from it because condemnation cuts you off at the knees to be who you really are: righteous. And you will never be who you truly are and do the exploits with your name on them, when you buy into condemnation.

You are clean, Beloved. You are righteous. And you are wildly loved! You are never forgotten or overlooked in favor of a more important sibling.

Who are you? You're your Father's son/daughter – His pride and His ecstatic joy. You're your Elder Brother's favorite sibling. You're your Husband's beloved wife. You're Holy Spirit's delight. Heaven rejoiced when you were born, because finally Love was expressed in a totally unique way to a world starving to know its Creator. You were intermingled with Pappa's DNA. His glory was expressed yet again.

You were imprinted with His fingerprint and released to make your mark on a confused, hurting, and dying world.

4.
WHAT'S WRONG?

What's Wrong with Me? What's Wrong with You?

Life is a struggle. We live in a fallen world. The enemy of our souls is waging war against humanity to steal, kill, and destroy, reveling when he can use us to be destructive instruments against one another (John 10:10). Something is wrong. Many things are wrong. We live surrounded by a natural world of wrongness. What amazes me though, is that even in the midst of all the fallen-ness of the world, the beauty of and life in our world is irrepressible! The echoes of Love and visions of beauty, even when God is not recognized, are so loud and vivid one has to spend a lot of futile energy trying to stifle, mar, or misrepresent them. But the consciousness of Love all around can be suppressed. Many people have fallen asleep to His Presence.

With this I have found people fall into two camps. One camp struggles with this pervasive sense of wrongness and really feels that what is wrong is themselves. Their question is a nagging, "What is wrong with me?" They focus on their shortcomings, their sins, their muffin top, their muffin bottom, their impatience with the kids, their temper, their addictions, their crazy thoughts – the list is endless.

The other camp has the perspective that there's something definitely wrong and that expressly rests with someone or everyone else. Their question is, "What is wrong with you?" Then usually they will be happy to tell you just what is wrong with you and everyone else – in living color! They focus on others' shortcomings, others' sins, others' muffin tops and bottoms, others' impatience with the kids, those misbehaving kids, others' tempers, others' addictions, others' crazy thoughts – that list is endless. They are not fun to be around.

And then there is God. He lives and inhabits peace. He is the Prince of Peace (Isaiah 9:6) where there is nothing missing and nothing broken. Peace here is the Hebrew word *shalom*, which includes: completeness, soundness, welfare, safety, soundness (in body), health, prosperity, quiet, tranquility, peace from war, contentment in human relationships, and relationship with God. That is quite a job description! Love is completely self-sustained. When He is unveiled or manifested, wrong things become right. The unseen ever-present realm of heaven is unveiled on earth in a tangible way just as Jesus prayed (Matthew 6:10).

We instinctively know that heaven is good. That is, unless we have run into a religious misrepresentation of God and heaven that is heavy, hard, condemning, scary, or simply boring. Perhaps life has lied to us that God is hard, absent, passive, or wimpy. Whether we admit it or not, we still long for heaven. But according to the Gospel, heaven is inside the believer and "at our fingertips." Jesus and His work on the cross totally singlehandedly reconciled the whole world back to God (2 Corinthians 5:18-19). We were made as spiritual beings to dwell inside a physical body as one with Christ (1 Corinthians 6:17).

GOD MADE US IN HIS IMAGE TO EXPRESS HIS GLORY AND MANIFEST HEAVEN AROUND US.

We were designed to simultaneously inhabit heaven even as we walk around the earth realm (Ephesians 2:6). What a mystery!

God made us in His image to express His glory and manifest heaven around us. But if we are rejecting ourselves or rejecting others because there is "something wrong" with us or others, we have totally missed the point. We have fallen for the lie of the enemy that people – ourselves or others – are problems. People are not problems. People are not projects to work on. You're not a project to work on. People are treasures even if they are causing a lot of problems. You are a treasure, even if you are causing a lot of problems.

And let's face it, we all have and will continue to cause problems sometimes when we are trying the hardest not to. That is why we need a Savior. That is why *everyone* needs a Savior. It is a level playing ground. Because toil as we might, we can never overcome our own weakness and fallenness in and of ourselves. At the root of that fallenness is spiritual disconnect, or a perceived one, that manifests in our minds, wills, emotions, bodies, behavior, and situations around us. Most of the Church has never learned or has forgotten that Jesus took care of ALL that, including that old fallen Adamic nature. The second Adam, Jesus, did an overwhelmingly better job at masterfully, sweepingly, and irrevocably redeeming a fallen world and human race than the first Adam did at precipitating the fall of that world and the human race (Romans 5 & 6 [just marinate in both chapters, yum!]; 2 Corinthians 5:16-18; Ephesians 4:21-23; Colossians 3:8-10). But most of the Church, not to mention the world, is much better acquainted with the effects of the fall than the effects of the cross.

Help Me!

We need help, and we never outgrow our need for help as sophisticated as we might become. That is why God sent Holy Spirit to inhabit and move through the believer. Holy Spirit is busy bringing all things back to God, to bring all things back to Love (Colossians 1:20). And Love is not the least bit intimidated by our big, fat, hairy problems. He continues to go about the work of manifesting us – digging out, cutting out, cleaning up, polishing, and then unveiling the diamonds we were made to be. It is not a comfortable process. Can anyone relate?

But God is not really focused on our comfort or discomfort at being conformed to His image – the image of Love. Our running, rebellion, whining, and complaining don't slow Him down in the least. He knows that the end result of submitting to Love will be powerful, amazing, and glorious. Like a parent who knows school is needed for a kid who hates school, God sees the sweeping long-term picture personally and throughout the ages and is unwilling to leave us alone. He is unwilling to allow us to settle for less than who we were created to be. He is unwilling to let you be less than who you were created to be.

LOVE IS NOT THE LEAST BIT INTIMIDATED BY OUR BIG, FAT, HAIRY PROBLEMS. HE CONTINUES TO GO ABOUT THE WORK OF UNVEILING THE DIAMONDS WE WERE MADE TO BE.

On the flip side, God does not coerce or control. He does not have to. Fear seeks to control and manipulate. Just think of all the controlling people in your life. Some of you may see yourself (or you may need to get a clue). The need to control is based out of fear. Love is the direct opposite of fear. Love has a zero-tolerance policy for fear. Like light vs. darkness, Love takes up all the space as fear flees. Scripture actually says that Love casts out the fear and the torment that comes with it (1 John 4:17-18). I love the way The Message Version puts it:

God is love. When we take up permanent residence in a life of love, we live in God, and God lives in us. This way, love has the run of the house, becomes at home and mature in us, so that we're free of worry on Judgment Day – our standing in the world is identical with Christ's. There is no room in love for fear. Well-formed love banishes fear. Since fear is crippling, a fearful life fear of death, fear of judgment is one not yet fully formed in love.

LOVE IS UNWILLING TO LET YOU BE LESS THAN WHO YOU WERE CREATED TO BE.

Instead of fear, Love gives us power, love, and a sound mind with discipline and self-control (2 Timothy 1:7). That is where control is legitimate and completely appropriate: self-control! Self-control is supernatural and a fruit of Love. In controlling ourselves, we express Love and put Him on display. That draws the world to Christ.

Ever heard "You will know them by their love for one another?" Yeah, I thought so. We are not known by our miracles or good works. We are known by our love and to the extent that our miracles and good works are an expression of Love; that is really great public relations for the kingdom and God we represent. Love pursues, entreats, compels, courts, persuades, and fascinates with a holy passion for the objects of His desire.

Love is intoxicating. Love is hard to resist. But resist we often do. Like rebellious stubborn little children, we have all run off on our own. We have all run headlong into some foolish destructive path, often over and over again. We have all been foolish, saying in our hearts "there is no God" (Proverbs 14:11, 53:1) at some time or another. We have all, as Proverbs 26:11 graphically portrays, returned to the vomit of our own destructiveness. We want to do what we want to do, when we want to do it, and we want to do it our way. I hear a Frank Sinatra song coming on.

LOVE HAS A ZERO-TOLERANCE POLICY FOR FEAR.

Many of us have called that "independence" and celebrated it. But foolishness is still foolishness even with a sexy label slapped over the top. The Bible does not mince words or spare egos. Psalm 14:1-2 (TLB) says,

> *That man is a fool who says to himself, There is no God! Anyone who talks like that is warped and evil and cannot really be a good person at all.*

Wow! How many of you have been offended by the word of God? The Gospel is an equal opportunity offender. Truly, Jesus offended people all the time – particularly the ones who were sure they were righteous based on their own merits. It got Him crucified!

Anything less than depending totally on Christ's free gift of righteousness to be "right" and to act right is self-righteousness. Indeed Christ said apart from Him we could do nothing (John 15:5). Talk about offensive – who do you think you are, Jesus? But in fact, Jesus was compelled to become sin that we might be made His righteousness (2 Corinthians 5:21). It was an unfair trade at Jesus's expense. But Love was glad to ante up. The word of God says that it was for the joy set before Him (read "you") He endured the cross (Hebrews 12:12). It was *personal!*

So What Are You Going to Do?

Whatever we focus on magnifies.

If you are not convinced, remember back when you were a teenager and to your horror you discovered that you had developed a big zit right before a party, prom, date, or get-together with your friends? You put on all the acne potions and perhaps used a cover stick. You obsessed in front of the mirror, returning every hour to see if it had shrunk. And when it came time to make your social entry, you were sure the entire world was zeroed in on your zit. As a matter of fact, it felt that your zit, not you, was making its entry into a room of social critics. Essentially you *were* your zit, and shame and embarrassment cloaked you.

WHATEVER WE FOCUS ON MAGNIFIES.

If you mentioned it to a friend, it was likely they said something like, "Oh yeah, I guess can see that." But they didn't really see it or think much of it prior to you mentioning it. They were too busy focusing on their fat stomach or funky hair or social awkwardness. You remember, I am sure. Oh, the anti-joy of those pre-teen and teenage trials.

The point: from zits to sin to beauty to God – whatever you focus on becomes magnified in your mind. And as it becomes magnified in your mind, it becomes empowered. In the case of the zit, the magnifying empowered shame and embarrassment.

And the word of God says that as a man thinks in his heart so is he (Proverbs 23:7).

This is why scripture says to be transformed by the renewing of your mind (Romans 12:2). Notice it is an inside-out job. It doesn't say "be transformed by prayer, fasting, Bible study, confessing the Word, worship, attending a service or conference, or even reading this book (truth in advertising)." These are all wonderful and necessary disciplines and activities – especially the book part (shameless plug). But the transformation process that we are after will only happen if those disciplines and activities result in our minds being renewed to think the way God thinks about ourselves and our situations. Otherwise, we had a great time (or not), but we walk out of that time essentially the same way we walked in. Our zit still seems huge!

But this does not have to be you!

There are times we have to get radical in our minds. We have to fight the good fight of faith (1 Timothy 6:12). We have to take every thought captive to the standard of Christ and make them bow to that. The word says the following in 2 Corinthians 10:3-5 (AMP):

> **THERE ARE TIMES WE HAVE TO GET RADICAL IN OUR MINDS.**

> *For though we walk in the flesh [as mortal men], we are not carrying on our [spiritual] warfare according to the flesh and using the weapons of man. The weapons of our warfare are not physical [weapons of flesh and blood].*
> *Our weapons are divinely powerful for the destruction of fortresses. We are destroying sophisticated arguments and every exalted and proud thing that sets itself up against the [true] knowledge of God, and we are taking every thought and purpose captive to the obedience of Christ.*

What did God say? What did He *not* say? You get to decide what you are going to agree with and what you are going to magnify. You get to decide what you are not going to agree with and what you are going to dismiss.

Are you going to magnify the zit? Or are you going to magnify that you are loved, loveable, competent, and attractive, and magnify the party and people around you?

Only then are you free to enjoy the party.

The silliness of this example is by design. At the end of the day, anything that we magnify that is not in line with what God said is foolishness, because we just took God out of the equation in our minds. Remember, a fool in his heart says there is no God (Psalm 14:1; 53:1).

God has said very definite things about that sickness, financial crisis, relational fallout, emotional roller coaster, and accusation. He has more to say and show for those who have ears to hear and eyes to see. Often when we are not seeing/hearing/connecting with God about the trials in our lives, it is because we have allowed the trial to be magnified and God to be shrunk in our minds. And that is where the battle for your faith and your promises are.

Galatians 6:9 (KJV) says:

> *And let us not be weary in well doing: for in due season we shall reap, if we faint not.*

Where do you think you faint or give up? You do so in your mind first. If you fainted, you just fell for the enemy and his deception. Remember the first temptation the serpent held out was, "Did God say?" I like the New International Version, which says:

> *Now the serpent was more crafty than any of the wild animals the Lord God had made. He said to the woman, Did God really say, "You must not eat from any tree in the garden?" (Genesis 3:1)*

He's been using that same tired line throughout the millennia. But the problem is, we are still falling for it. We allow him to cause us to faint in our minds, and we let go of the promises Love gave us. We've stopped fixing our eyes on Love (Hebrews 12:2), the One Who is the Author and perfect Finisher of our faith. We've allowed ourselves to get distracted and hoodwinked.

THE ENEMY OF OUR SOUL HAS BEEN USING THAT SAME TIRED LINE THROUGHOUT THE MILLENNIA. BUT THE PROBLEM IS, WE ARE STILL FALLING FOR IT.

The New Living Translation says in Hebrews 10:35-36:

> *So do not throw away this confident trust in the Lord. Remember the great reward it brings you! Patient endurance is what you need now so that you will continue to do God's will. Then you will receive all that he has promised.*

God's response to having to find Adam and his wife hiding in the bushes awkwardly trying to slap fig leaves over their nakedness is very telling:

> *"Who told you that you were naked?" the Lord God asked. (Genesis 3:11 NLT)*

Clearly, nakedness had not entered their minds prior to this. Aha!

What voice had they been listening to? The serpent's. What voice have you been listening to? What have you been listening to and magnifying in your own mind that has let the problem seem huge, the enemy seem huge, and you seem small and God seem small? When this happens, we have allowed the enemy to get away with literal murder. It's time to get flat out ticked off and rebel against what the enemy has been putting over on you!

So Where the Hell Were You?

I like to use the "H" word, because it accurately reflects our hearts many times. And, by the way, it is not a curse word. Jesus used it appropriately quite a bit (Matthew 5:22, 29-30; 7:13; 10:28, 16:18; 18:9; 23:15,33). I love the way He made no bones about things and while He did walk on water, He refused to walk on religious eggshells. Moreover, referring to satan's dwelling place does not empower him in the least. He is so pathetic in his defeated state, he doesn't even have the keys to his own house (Revelation 1:18). No wonder he has to use smoke and mirror deception to wreak havoc!

The enemy's MO has always been stealing, killing, and destroying (John 10:10). And when he does, we often get offended with God instead of the culprit! satan loves this. It is his pathetic way to try to get back at God and destroy us in the process. And we fall for it in droves. Yes, I know so many of us are good little Christians and we would never be mad at God for not doing this or seeming to do that. The truth is, however, we do not really function out of our logical brains, even if those brains may know a ton of scripture affirming that God is perfect and sinless. The area of logic is the area of the neocortex. However, we primarily functionally live out of our emotional and often subconscious minds that are connected to the emotional part of our brains – the limbic system. The limbic system is reflexive and functions much quicker than our neocortex. So consciously we may not be aware that we are offended with God, but we are often very offended at God, or at someone who represented God to us and failed us.

We need to come clean with the fact that so many of us are disappointed with, mad at, or disillusioned with God. For many, it comes as a huge surprise when the Lord reveals it to us, because we are not consciously aware. We may not feel anger, but wherever we are compromised in our hearts we are offended, and it

> MANY OF US NEED TO FORGIVE A SINLESS GOD NOT BECAUSE HE SINNED, BUT BECAUSE WE ARE INJURED IN OUR HEARTS.

needs to be released in forgiveness. I see this operating practically daily in wonderful godly people.

Jesus said, "Offense will come" (Matthew 18:7). The subconscious and sometimes not-so-subconscious parts of ourselves are often screaming: "Where the hell were You, God?" "You promised me and didn't deliver." "I did everything You asked in faith, and You didn't have my back." "You let my _____ die/get molested/get cancer/get in a crippling accident." "How could You let my business/my life's work fail?" "How could You leave me high and dry?" The list goes on.

LOVE IS NOT OFFENDED AT OUR OFFENSE.

Yes, folks, so many of us need to forgive a sinless God – not because He sinned, but because we are injured in our hearts. And I'll say it again, heart injury is the essence of offense, whether or not you feel ticked. And here is where some of our breakdown in our functional connection with God often comes from: we don't want to hear, see, connect with, or receive from people we are mad at or afraid of. And God is very much "people."

But God is Love, and Love is not easily offended. He is not offended at our offense. He just wants to help us get past it so we can connect with Him, get unstuck, and receive from Him. When we do come clean with all this, we can begin to hear/see/connect with Love so that we can receive the good things Love always intended.

The Accuser of the Brethren & Sistren

The problem when we focus on ourselves and our problems is we magnify what seems to be so wrong with us. When we focus on other people and their problems, we magnify what seems to be wrong with them. The word of God says that satan is a liar and the father of lies (John 8:44) and he is also the accuser of our brothers and sisters. He interestingly accuses us before God day and night (Revelation 12:10). he has a huge chip on his shoulder. The word of God calls this hatred "enmity" and says the following about it:

> *And I will put enmity (open hostility) between you and the woman, and between your seed (offspring) and her Seed; He shall [fatally] bruise your head, And you shall [only] bruise His heel. (Genesis 3:15 AMP)*

This is an open hostility that does not lessen but intensifies over time. satan is the original misogynist (woman hater). he is the original architect of the oppression of women, which has gone on since the fall and still goes on. But let's be clear, he hates *everyone* created in the image of God. He hates men too and is their oppressor as well. When anyone is oppressed, we are all oppressed. We were made to be one in Christ (Ephesians 4:4, 25).

What is my point? The main one is that satan roams about like a roaring lion seeking whom he may devour (1 Peter 5:8), and his main tactic is to deceive, to lure into sin, and then to condemn, steal, kill, and destroy.

He trips you into sin and then he beats you up, accusing and condemning you and, then, often gets you to accuse and condemn yourself. You start doing his job for him. When we receive condemnation or condemn ourselves, we are powerless to overcome the very sin that entraps us. The mocking voices come. The torment amplifies, and we become hopeless.

But Love – Love couldn't help Himself, and He can't help Himself. Jesus came to die for the sins of the *whole world* (1 John 2:2). No one is excluded or left out. Jesus came to set things right. Jesus came to set us right. And that happy subject is all wrapped up in the oh-so-unbelievably good news of the Gospel – the real version. There are a lot of funky, religious, adulterated versions that stink. Religion always stinks. But when we dive into and splash and romp around Love's ecstatic response to our hopeless human condition, it is a thing of freedom, joy, and beauty!

RELIGION ALWAYS STINKS.

We will romp some more in the next chapter. So put on your "oh-so-flattering" bathing suits and get ready to plunge into the center of Love's ooey-gooey goodness. You can even skinny dip – naked and unashamed! Whoo-hoo!

Love Encounter Break #4

Let's take a break to encounter Love and have Him reveal where you have been carrying condemnation, or a message that something is wrong with you, or that you are not enough or are too much.

Pappa, I agree with the one reading this right now for the grace to rest and receive from You! You made them in Love, but the world does not always operate in love. The world criticizes, rejects and condemns.

So right now I ask that You show this one reading in a word or words, thoughts, pictures, feelings, impressions, a knowing, or however else You want to manifest how there has been distortion with who they are and how they feel about themselves.

I thank You that You are in the midst of every bit of this process and ask that if they need more help, to connect them exactly with the safe, effective help they need.

Now let yourself relax and let Love speak in those words, thoughts, pictures, feelings, impressions, knowings, or other manifestations, where you have been carrying condemnation or a message or messages that something is wrong with you or that you are not enough or are too much.

Jot down anything you are getting, however small, even if you are not sure it is God. You can review this later or bring it to a trusted spiritual leader to help you judge it.

_____

_____

_____

_____

_____

_____

Relax. Let God do the heavy lifting. Let Him surprise you. Be patient with yourself if this is new. He will help you! You will get better and better at this as you practice! If at any time this really does not feel safe to do, shut it down, and you can go back later when you are in a better place. But if Love is asking you to push through your fears so He can minister to them, heed that.

If you need more space, grab or make a new journal.

How have I been brainwashed that there is something wrong with me or that I am guilty and condemnable? (These are lies that feel like truth.):

_____

_____

_____

_____

_____

_____

_____

Let me pray:

> *Pappa, thank You for revealing this lie/these lies. What truth do You want to show them?*

Truth Love is giving me about myself and my life:

_____

_____

_____

_____

Let me pray:

> *Thank You, Pappa, for revealing this to your kids. If they need to forgive themselves and/or others, please bring up those people in their minds and help them with the grace to do this.*

Keep in mind you may not feel angry, but the issue is not anger, it is an offense that is still there. Remember, you are not saying people who harmed you deserve to be forgiven, you are not saying things were OK, and you do not have to reconcile with a toxic person. Also, you don't have to feel like it – just be obedient. This is for your freedom!

If you feel you have already done this, trust Him that He knows what He is doing.

If you are sensing people (including yourself and God), start by saying, "As an act of my will, I choose to forgive _____ for _____." (And let her rip in full technicolor. This is not the time to be "nice" or come up with the reasons why "they" couldn't help it. It is safe and healthy for you to get toxicity out of you.)

If others come up in your mind to forgive, do the same with them until you feel the forgiveness issue is released for this time.

Let me pray:

Pappa, show Your kids what truth You want to minister to them.

Write it down below.

The truth Love is giving me about myself or others (now that I have released them/myself in forgiveness):

_____

_____

_____

If you are still not connecting to God as Love, ask Him, what lie am I believing about You or myself that is hindering me connecting to You here?

_____

Let me pray:

Pappa, what truth do You want to show them about that lie?

Write down what you get. Keep in mind there may be a series of lies that you may need to take the time to let Him deal with, so repeat this as much as necessary.

_____

_____

_____

_____

_____

_____

Once you go through those lies and receive truth(s), let me pray:

Pappa, thank You for helping your kids! I thank You, Holy Spirit, for leading each and every person into the Truth of who they are, created in Your Love, holy and blameless before the foundation of the world.

I thank You, Pappa, and I ask You again, on behalf of these, for heaven to invade earth right here, right now, right where each and every person is. I thank You for fabulous life-giving encounters of their oneness with You, You in them, and them in You, and helping each and every person enter in to those encounters and keeping them safe!

Write down what you get.

_____

_____

_____

_____

_____

_____

If you are still struggling, you are probably needing some healing and help with this. You are totally not alone – this is quite common, and with help this gets easier and easier, so you will be a pro! Know that I am actively standing with you and for you in this and am trusting Love to lead you exactly where you need to go to get the help you need and the help He wants to provide for you! He is masterful at this and is and will be for you! I trust Him implicitly with you and for you!

5.
WHAT'S RIGHT?

Jar Loot

The word of God calls us treasure in jars of clay (2 Corinthians 4:7). The treasure is us, and God is in us. The believer is inextricably united with God. The word of God in 1 Corinthians 6:17 (Voice) says:

> But when you are joined with the Lord, you become one spirit with Him.

Apparently God does not find you or those around you distasteful.

Apparently He is so enthralled with people that He chose to become one with them, whether they know it or accept it or not. And He has permanently tied the knot (Ephesian 5:31-32). He has so united Himself with the believer that in the spirit where you begin and end is mixed up with where He begins and ends.

The enemy of our souls is constantly trying to hoodwink believers into believing they are separate from God. If he can do that, he takes the believer out of rest and into toiling for something that they already are and something they already have simply by inheritance.

> LOVE IS SO ENTHRALLED WITH PEOPLE THAT HE CHOSE TO BECOME ONE WITH THEM, WHETHER THEY KNOW IT OR ACCEPT IT OR NOT. AND HE HAS PERMANENTLY TIED THE KNOT.

When we look at ourselves and others as problems, who have problems, we magnify what problems exist. Our mountains become mountain ranges and threaten to overcome us, rather than us overcoming our mountains. When we come out of the perspective of our oneness with God, we lose our confidence in the One Who loved us and gave everything up for us (Galatians 2:20). It becomes about us trying to figure it out and do something.

Let's be clear, there is much to do. But when we operate separately from God, we cannot hear clearly what we should do as partners with God. We are functioning out of a place of deficit, with the illusion that the solution was not already released two thousand years ago. On Calvary, Jesus completed His task, as a man and as mankind, and pronounced, "It is finished" (John 19:30). The word "finished" is *teleo* in the Greek and means "complete, execute, conclude, discharge (a debt), accomplish, make an end, expire, fill up, finish, go over, pay, and perform."

Jesus had His Father's assignment to complete as a man, born in the flesh but without sin, empowered by Holy Spirit. That assignment reconciled the entire world back to the Father and reestablished a race of sons of God and co-heirs, whose assignment is to manifest the kingdom of Heaven on earth (Colossians 1:20-21; Romans 8:14-18; Matthew 6:10).

When we get out of rest, we act as if there is something left that still needs to be completed. In effect we are saying, "Jesus, thanks for all that cross stuff. I'm glad I'm not going to hell, but You don't know how I'm suffering down here, and I'm freaking out." Jesus didn't "miss a spot." He covered everything it took to reclaim back the entire human race and the world that had fallen. The beauty of it is that He moves through you and me to take back what satan stole. That is justice and that is recompense!

> WHEN WE GET OUT OF REST, WE ACT AS IF THERE IS SOMETHING LEFT THAT STILL NEEDS TO BE COMPLETED... JESUS DIDN'T "MISS A SPOT."

But getting there from here in whatever particular area is plaguing you requires the "work" of believing. The Amplified Version of John 6:28-30 says:

> *Then they asked Him, "What are we to do, so that we may habitually be doing the works of God?" Jesus answered, "This is the work of God: that you believe [adhere to, trust in, rely on, and have faith] in the One whom He has sent."*

Believing requires confidence in God. If you believe that something is wrong with you, you are self-condemned, and it is very hard to believe that your prayers will manifest. Hebrews 10:35 (KJV) says:

> *Cast not away therefore your confidence, which hath great recompense of reward.*

WE HAVE BEEN MARKED BY LOVE WITH THE RIGHTEOUSNESS OF LOVE.

First John 3:20-21 in the New King James Version brings out the connection between the status of our hearts and our confidence toward God:

> *For if our heart condemns us, God is greater than our heart, and knows all things. Beloved, if our heart does not condemn us, we have confidence toward God.*

I love this verse because it says that even if we feel condemned, God knows our hearts and is greater than our hearts. Jesus, in the flesh, experienced where we are at and He has compassion on us and is well able to help us and put us over (Hebrews 2:18; 4:15). The "it" in the "it is finished" portion applies here. Although Jesus was sinless, He actually became the entity of sin so that we would be made His righteousness by faith (1 Corinthians 5:21; Romans 3:22). What a deal! Our righteousness is His righteousness. We have been marked by Love with the righteousness of Love. But we really had nothing to do with this exchange. We are righteous, but the Source of our righteousness is only found exclusively in Love without any additional help on our part.

Because making us His righteousness cost Love so much, it makes our efforts at doing "our part" in the righteousness equation reek (Isaiah 64:6). It is called self-righteousness, which is really a form of sneaky pride that takes its own credit. What an affront to God (Romans 3:21-23; Galatians 2:21; Philippians 3:9)! However, Love is so lovely, His is not easily angered and keeps no records of wrongs (1 Corinthians 13:4). The self-righteous person is forgiven, but that person does cut himself or herself off from the grace of God. This is not a punishment. It is because they are acting out of a spirit of independence that keeps them from depending on Love, the ultimate Source of all good things (James 1:17)!

You don't have to be a Bible scholar or even to have ever picked a Bible up to be turned off by a self-righteous person. And let's be clear, self-righteousness does not just come in a Christian variety (although there's plenty there and most believers have been guilty of this in one way or another). How many of you have been nauseated by self-righteousness coming from other religions, and from things that are not considered religious but really are systems of religion: zealous diet and exercise adherents, zealous environmentalists, zealous political adherents, zealous intellectualism...you get the drift?

With many very good things in my upbringing, I was also brought up with an overwhelming condemnation of never being good enough with intellectual performance, playing the violin and piano, eating a self-denying diet, artistic endeavors, and the list unfortunately went on. There was the self-righteousness of elitism in being academic and well-cultured. I had had encounters with Jesus really since I could remember, but I had never heard the Gospel and didn't know this "man" I encountered except

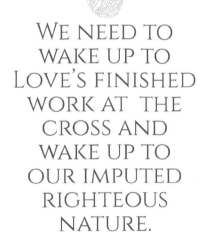

WE NEED TO WAKE UP TO LOVE'S FINISHED WORK AT THE CROSS AND WAKE UP TO OUR IMPUTED RIGHTEOUS NATURE.

that He loved me and I loved Him. I was so drawn to the churches I would visit with my friends and to the Bible, but I was too ashamed to reveal to my family that was my heart. The unconditional acceptance and love I had felt in those encounters were my true self and heart. But I was under the law in my home and the striving for acceptance and love that I could never attain. I was trying to earn righteousness amidst a shame I could not shake. Being under the law and the condemnation that followed, came from a self-righteousness that didn't know any better. And that portion stunk. So I have compassion for people under the weight of condemnation, and a heart to set people free from that bondage!

While we do not earn our righteousness, we do have a part to play. We need to wake up to Love's finished work at the cross and wake up to our imputed righteous nature. The word *impute* here, means "to credit to a person or a cause" ("Merriam-Webster Online Dictionary"). We need to wake up to who we really are. When we do that, we will be empowered to shake off sin and the condemnation that goes with it, like a false skin that does not fit anymore.

The Classic Amplified Version says it like this in 1 Corinthians 15:34:

> *Awake [from your drunken stupor and return] to sober sense and your right minds, and sin no more. For some of you have not the knowledge of God [you are utterly and willfully and disgracefully ignorant, and continue to be so, lacking the sense of God's presence and all true knowledge of Him]. I say this to your shame.*

It is non-negotiable in the Christian walk to camp out and get our righteousness and our blamelessness before God experientially integrated into our very beings. If we constantly feel unworthy when Love has made us worthy, then we will constantly function as paupers and orphans in one way or another. Paupers and orphans beg and strive for everything they get. We are kings, priests, sons, and daughters (1 Peter 2:5, 9; Romans 5:17; 8:16-19) and we have an inheritance provided by the grace of God through faith (Romans 4:16; Ephesians 2:8). If that is not integrated into the substance of our experienced identity, we will act like we have to earn something that Love sacrificed to give us without measure before we knew we ever would need it.

IF LOVE HAS A PROBLEM, IT IS BECAUSE WE SIMPLY DO NOT BELIEVE THAT HE IS AS GOOD AS HE TRULY IS.

We do not see God rightly when we see Him as holding out because we are not good enough or do not do enough well enough. If Love has a problem, it is because we simply do not believe that He is as good as He truly is.

Love is wooing the heart of an unbelieving world and convicting the heart of an unbelieving church.

We do not believe in a real sense that we are as good as He truly made us to be. We do not totally believe that He truly provided for everything we would ever need for our situations and for a lost and dying world.

You Are Not a Problem

You are not a problem. You are as righteous as Jesus is, because Love made you so. Stifle the arguing and let Love convince you. The deal is that Love is the Source of everything including your righteousness. He has marked you with His love. He has marked you with His righteousness. The New Age world has hit on this intrinsic righteousness much better than the church in many ways, which is one of the big reasons that many former believers have left the church to join the New Age movement. Tragic! The churchy religious spirit, and the condemnation that comes with it when people are not able to "hit the mark," drives people away to seek acceptance and love

LOVE IS WOOING THE HEART OF AN UNBELIEVING WORLD AND CONVICTING THE HEART OF AN UNBELIEVING CHURCH.

elsewhere outside the church. The sad thing is that often the New Age, the gay community, Eastern religions, diet/exercise enthusiasts have done a better job at unconditional love and acceptance than the church. The church can learn a lot from those communities, if we will be humble enough and see through the eyes of love vs. judgment to do so.

God created each and every person, regardless of which artificial "community" they "belong" to. In truth, there is one race: the human race, created in the image and likeness of God. We can all learn from one another.

We don't have to be afraid of sin – that it will contaminate or defile us. We are intrinsically righteous, and we cannot be made unrighteous. We are holy and spread holiness. The idea that sin can con-taminate those who are separated unto Love is an old covenant idea. The ability of sin to contaminate righteousness is laughable! Are you kidding? That delusion insults the work of the cross, where the prin-ciple of sin itself was singlehandedly completely overmastered. How good a job did Christ do? How well is Love able to keep His own?

There is no fear in love. If we can learn from a rock or a tree or the animal kingdom or the stars that all speak of a glorious, love-ly Creator, we can certainly learn from people, who are created in Love's image but just do not know Him accurately and intimately and scripturally yet. We can learn from people sucked into the abyss of sin and "proud of it." And, yes, we can even learn from all the other denominations/church bodies that we may secretly be judging for not having it all together, like we think our particular pet denom-ination/church bodies has.

Sometimes, we, as the adorable, beautiful church, are so silly! That is why we need to repent (change the way we think) so we can be transformed and conformed into the image of Love (Romans 12:2; 8:29).

Humility is a beautiful thing. Love is humble.

HUMILITY IS A BEAUTIFUL THING. LOVE IS HUMBLE.

Jesus said,

Come to Me, all who are weary and heavily burdened [by religious rituals that provide no peace], and I will give you rest [refreshing your souls with salvation]. Take My yoke upon you and learn from Me [following Me as My disciple], for I am gentle and humble in heart, and you will find rest (renewal, blessed quiet) for your souls. (Matthew 11:28-29 AMP)

WE ARE SUPPOSED TO BE IDENTIFIABLE AND FAMOUS FOR OUR LOVE FOR ONE ANOTHER.

Jesus didn't argue with people or have to be right, although, just a guess, He probably had His theology straight. He is gentle and humble at heart and on earth He led sin-ridden people to discover truth, often through lovingly asking pointed questions that revealed the heart, while not judging them (John 4:1-29). The only people He really lambasted were the self-righteous, who were headed straight toward hell because they insisted they had earned their own righteousness (check out all of Mathew 23).

Since pride blinds, sometimes being hit by a righteous two-by-four is necessary to save us from our own folly. But Jesus was never prideful in the process. He never cut people down to make Himself appear better. He did and does cut down the foolish mindsets and the hypocritical behavior as He convicts us. But the purpose and drive are always love to ultimately "edify" (build up). And He calls us to love in the same way.

Remember, we are supposed to be identifiable and famous for our love for one another (John 13:35). And because the religious church can't "hit the self-righteous mark" either, it can easily flip into hypocrisy, which stinks even further. That has driven many away as well. Now Love does not condemn, but He does diagnose and will spank with conviction (Romans 8:1; John 16:7-11; Hebrews 12:11). When you are convicted by Holy Spirit, the first thing you are reminded of is that you have been made righteous and you are acting counter to your true identity. Love calls you up and out of that mess, and He empowers you to walk away. Ask me how I know.

Where the New Age movement has shipwrecked is that it considers people or the universe or cosmic consciousness as the source. All gods and roads lead to heaven. But everything was created by one God, in triune expression, Who is the Source of everything and is drawing everything back to Himself (Colossians 1:20; 2 Corinthians 5:18-19). And that God is Love.

The Church is marked by Love and is called to be ministers of reconciliation, releasing that reconciliation of the entire world back to Love (2 Corinthians 5:18-19). That means we are to receive God's love, love ourselves, love God back, and love one another. This is what we are supposed to be

WE ARE TO RECEIVE GOD'S LOVE, LOVE OURSELVES, LOVE GOD BACK, AND LOVE ONE ANOTHER.

famous for (John 13:34-35). That much love sloshing around represents a good God rightly. It is irresistible, especially if it proves solid, constant, and unwavering. It is the goodness of God that draws all men to change their minds about Who God really is and draws their hearts back to the One Who loves them (Romans 2:4).

You Are a Solution

You are not a problem. You are a solution who may have problems, but the problems don't have you!

God wants the unveiling of the solutions He already masterminded and accomplished for you, and He wants to use you as the conduit of those solutions for others around you.

> LOVE HAS CREATED A RACE OF CHAMPIONS, MOST OF WHOM HAVE NO CLUE WHO THEY REALLY ARE.

Your problems, while not created by God, can be used to release and build the intrinsic champion in you. Love has created a race of champions, most of whom have no clue who they really are (2 Corinthians 2:14; Romans 2:21; 8:37; 1 John 4:4; 5:4-5).

Love Encounter Break #5

Let's take another break to encounter Love and have Him reveal you as a solution for the world and a champion for Love.

Pappa, I agree with the one reading this right now for the grace to rest and receive from You! You made them in Love as a solution in a loveless confused world and a champion for You in You! So right now I ask that You show this one reading in a word or words, thoughts, pictures, feelings, impressions, a knowing or however else You want to manifest more about this reality of who You made them to be as a solution and a champion of Love. I thank You that You are helping them receive the beauty and glory of who You created them to be.

Now let yourself relax and let Love speak in those words, thoughts, pictures, feelings, impressions, knowings, or other manifestations of you as He created you to be – a solution in a loveless confused world and a champion for Love.

Jot down anything you are getting, however small. You know the drill. If you need more space, grab or make a new journal.

How have I been created as a solution and a champion for Love?

_____

_____

_____

_____

If you are having a hard time connecting with this reality, let me pray:

> *Pappa, help this one forgive themselves for everywhere they have not acted in line with being a solution and a champion for Love, if this is the issue. If this is not the issue, what is the lie that this one is believing that makes believing this truth hard? What is the truth You want them to know?*

The lie Love is revealing that I believe about myself and/or my life:

_____

_____

_____

_____

The truth Love is giving me about myself and my life:

_____

_____

_____

_____

_____

_____

_____

God wants us close and believing He is well-pleased with us. This allows faith to freely be released. It is easy to believe someone powerful will back you up when you just know they are wild about you.

> *Let us draw near with a true heart in full assurance of faith, having our hearts sprinkled from an evil conscience, and our bodies washed with pure water. (Hebrews 10:22 KJV)*

God has more good things for you, which are far above what you can possibly think, hope for, dare ask, or dream (Ephesians 3:20). This is why you are to use His faith, which He is the Author and Finisher of (Hebrews 12:2). This pleases Love because He actually gets to see those good things He provided for at His costly expense manifest in your life (Hebrews 11:6)!

When I was in residency training as a medical doctor, we were told that the first thing to do in a code blue situation is to stop and check your own pulse. When the emergencies of life hit you, as they do everyone, check your pulse first. God created that heart, which is pumping the blood that results in a pulse. It is reflective of the heart of a champion. The solutions you need – everything you need – comes from and through God.

LOVE IS YOUR SOURCE, AND HE HAS NOT MISSED NOR FORGOTTEN ANYTHING. HE IS NEVER STUMPED, STYMIED, OR RATTLED.

Love is your Source, and He has not missed nor forgotten anything. He is never stumped, stymied, or rattled. And Love does not hold out on the ones He loves.

So the next time the stuff hits the fan and you are at a loss, reconnect with the One Who loves you and gave Himself up for you (Galatians 2:20). Love gets to be Lord, not your problems or the enemy of our souls. When you are getting bullied by "What are you going to do?" shut that voice up by saying, "Absolutely nothing until I reconnect with God." He has all the strategies and grace to implement them. You, in the meantime, get to be an adored little child looking to your heavenly Daddy, knowing somehow, some brilliant way, He is going to put you over!

6.

THE OBJECT OF GOD'S PASSION

The Pleasure of God

God is Love (1 John 4:8). Central to my mandate in most everything I do, including writing this book, is to help you connect with God as Love, connect with who you are made in the image of Love, connect with your purpose to reveal and be a conduit of Love, and to be released and empowered with that purpose. It is a process of unveiling and discovery.

Love undergirds and is interlaced with the very reasons why you were born on planet Earth.

First and foremost, why you are here revolves around the pleasure of God (Psalms 147:11; Ephesians 1:5). You were made for the holy pleasure of God, Who is Love. You are His delight. He takes pleasure in you as His child, His friend, and His bride. God is not a demanding egomaniac, requiring that you do spiritual party tricks to serve Him, in order to please Him. He is easy to please, because He is a lover – He is Love.

> **YOU HAVE BEEN SO MARKED BY LOVE THAT YOUR VERY BEING IS IMPREGNATED WITH LOVE HIMSELF.**

You have been so marked by Love that your very being is impregnated with Love Himself. You are one with the Godhead by birth (1 Corinthians 6:17; Romans 6:3-6, 10). You are so intrinsically lovely and loveable, that you are a sheer joy for the triune Godhead, Who created you in His image and likeness (Genesis 1:26).

God explodes in song and dance when He thinks of you; He can't contain Himself!

> *Adonai, your God is in your midst – a mighty Savior! He will delight over you with joy. He will quiet you with His love. He will dance for joy over you with singing. (Zephaniah 3:16–18 TLV)*

You just can't help it. You are intrinsically adored and adorable! No wonder you please Him so much!

So, yes, you were very much created for His pleasure, but He is also the Source of everything good and pleasurable, with no downside.

The pleasure of sin is very real, but those pleasures are temporary (Hebrews 11:5). Sin carries the hangover of hard consequences that are not pleasant and are unavoidable apart from the mercy and the grace of God. But the pleasures of God have no downside. And He offers them freely.

James 1:16-18 says this in the Amplified Bible:

> Do not be misled, my beloved brothers and sisters. Every good thing given and every perfect gift is from above; it comes down from the Father of lights [the Creator and Sustainer of the heavens], in whom there is no variation [no rising or setting] or shadow cast by His turning [for He is perfect and never changes]. It was of His own will that He gave us birth [as His children] by the word of truth, so that we would be a kind of firstfruits of His creatures [a prime example of what He created to be set apart to Himself sanctified, made holy for His divine purposes].

GOD EXPLODES IN SONG AND DANCE WHEN HE THINKS OF YOU; HE CAN'T CONTAIN HIMSELF!

God's goodness is really good. When He created humankind, He put Adam in the Garden of Eden, which literally means garden of "pleasure" in the Hebrew.

And God is not stingy with the pleasure He makes available. But He is jealous for you and wants to be the ultimate Source of the pleasure He made you to enjoy!

I love 1 Timothy 6:17 (AMP), which says,

As for the rich in this present world, instruct them not to be conceited and arrogant, nor to set their hope on the uncertainty of riches, but on God, who richly and ceaselessly provides us with everything for our enjoyment.

He truly is a God of pleasure – His pleasure and ours.

Psalm 16:11 (NIV) says,

You make known to me the path of life; you will fill me with joy in your presence, with eternal pleasures at your right hand.

> LOVE IS JEALOUS FOR YOU AND WANTS TO BE THE ULTIMATE SOURCE OF THE PLEASURE HE MADE YOU TO ENJOY!

His Kingdom is all about righteousness, peace, and joy (Romans 14:17). He truly is a happy God, Who is all about manifesting His goodness. He wants happy kids. And, if you are a good parent, you want happy kids as well. But how many of you know that spoiling your kids with what they are convinced will make them happy will result in very unhappy kids, teens, and adults.

The word of God says that foolishness is bound up in the heart of children, who really do need and will thrive on godly wise correction, given in love out of a heart of honor (Proverbs 22:15; Hebrews 12:11; Ephesians 6:4).

Sometimes we know what we want, but we do not know what we really need (Romans 8:26). That is one reason why Love is always interceding for us (Romans 8:26, 34; Hebrews 7:25). How good do you think God is at praying for you? Cool beans! And He is happy while He is doing it.

We have all met people that we don't really want to ask how they are doing, because we just know they are going to unload on us and we'll walk away depressed or wanting to take a shower. But God is never like that. I always love to ask Him how He is doing. He is the most positive person I know! He always gives a wonderful

LOVE HAD TO EXPLODE IN THE FLAVOR OF EACH AND EVERY ONE OF US.

upbeat response. Even when He is grieved, it is because one of His kids is hurting or in danger. It is then I can partner with Him to intercede for others or just receive if it is about me. As we mature and grow up, bathing in His love, we can love Him back and minister to Him out of that love.

You Are the Object of God's Passion

The object of God's passion – yes, that is you, whether you can relate to that or not. He was unwilling to do without you. Before the foundation of the world, love overflowed within the Godhead. God wanted a family to lavish that love on and enjoy. He couldn't hold

Himself in. Love had to explode in the flavor of each and every one of us.

God's desire was to manifest Himself specifically through you in your flavor. You are irreplaceable. When you don't manifest, there is a hole in the universe that affects each and every person on the planet. We are all connected, because we were all made for a specific purpose and to reflect a specific dimension of our Creator. Those purposes are intertwined. Those facets of Love that we reflect combine together synergistically to reflect the fullness of Love. He is the Source of us and the Source of everything.

The New Age Movement got this right. We are all connected. They just don't recognize it is all tied up with Christ and Him alone. Love is drawing all things to Himself as the Source of everything and everyone. Colossians 1:19-20 (TLB) says,

> LOVE IS DRAWING ALL THINGS TO HIMSELF AS THE SOURCE OF EVERYTHING AND EVERYONE.

For God wanted all of himself to be in his Son. It was through what his Son did that God cleared a path for everything to come to him – all things in heaven and on earth – for Christ's death on the cross has made peace with God for all by his blood.

Ephesians 1:10 in The Message Version says,

He thought of everything, provided for everything we could possibly need, letting us in on the plans he took such delight in making. He set it all out before us in Christ, a long-range plan in which everything would be brought together and summed up in him, everything in deepest heaven, everything on planet earth.

Hunkering versus Occupying

Much of the body of Christ is operating in so much fear and oppression that it is all they can do to just make it through. But God's plan is not that we hunker down until we "make it" to heaven. He is Love, and perfect love makes no allowance for fear. First John 4:18 in the New American Standard Bible version says:

There is no fear in love; but perfect love casts out fear, because fear involves punishment, and the one who fears is not perfected in love.

He never made us to live under the circumstances. He made us more than conquerors, who are designed and empowered to overcome the circumstances that are arrayed against us (2 Corinthians 2:14; Romans 8:37; 12:21; 1 John 4:4; 5:4-5; Revelation 12:11). And understand, He never designed us to do any of this in our own strength. We are not supposed to pull ourselves up by our bootstraps, muster up our faith, and pull out our own strength.

Philippians 2:13 (AMP) elaborates:

For it is [not your strength, but it is] God Who is effectively at work in you, both to will and to work [that is, strengthening, energizing, and creating in you the longing and the ability to fulfill your purpose] for His good pleasure.

You were created for dependency. Jesus even said that apart from Him we can do no thing of eternal value (John 15:5). That is very scary if you do not/did not have a parent, friend, or spouse that has/had your back.

But the truth is, whether or not you can connect to it totally, you are to depend upon an immeasurably good, immeasurably powerful God, Who never leaves you nor forsakes you and Who is wildly

LOVE NEVER MADE US TO LIVE UNDER THE CIRCUMSTANCES.

smitten with you. You can afford to be that little child who the kingdom of Heaven belongs to (Matthew 19:14). Every place where it has felt that God did not come through and you are on your own, God can and wants to heal. We connect to the kingdom of Heaven with childlike faith and dependency, and we can engage the conflict with the kingdom of darkness as grown sons and daughters.

We are called to occupy the earth realm until He comes back, and to expand His kingdom by progressively transforming earth into heaven (Luke 19:14; Matthew 6:10). But in order to occupy and expand His kingdom, we must continue in this place of dependence. Apart from Love, we can do nothing of eternal consequence (John 15:5).

In the winter of 2011, I had a vision that really magnified that reality to me. I was with Jesus on the banks of a river of molten gold lava. I knew that we were in hell, and I was anxious to learn why we were there. We were communicating by our thoughts, and I knew that I was supposed to jump into this molten gold lava river. I was not very happy about it. I looked at Jesus asking Him if He was going to go with me. He didn't say anything, so I knew that was the wrong question. Finally, I blurted out, "Jesus is it going to be OK?!?" At that He reeled around, grabbed me by the shoulders, and locked eyes with me, His endless deep gorgeous eyes penetrating my very being. They said, "Catherine, you *know* Me!"

YOU WERE CREATED TO DEPEND UPON AN IMMEASURABLY GOOD, IMMEASURABLY POWERFUL GOD, WHO NEVER LEAVES YOU NOR FORSAKES YOU AND WHO IS WILDLY SMITTEN WITH YOU.

That was all I needed. I agreed, "Yup, I know You!" With that, I hiked up my skirt and jumped right into the middle of the river. Why I was wearing a skirt in hell and why I felt the need to hike it up to jump into molten gold lava, I have no idea. When Jesus is with you, there is humor in hell. But the moment my head went underneath the surface, BAM, we were back on the banks of the river. Except now it was completely transformed. The river was crystal clear with a waterfall to the left. There was a glorious garden teeming with life. As I took it all in, I heard Jesus, at my right side, say, "Because you were willing to die to yourself, I have given you the power to transform hell into the Garden of Eden!" Bam! I was awake and knew something really big had happened.

I understand that each one of us has a different flavor of calling. But let's be clear, we are *all* called to manifest heaven on earth the way Jesus taught in Matthew 6:11. The word manifest means "readily be perceived by the senses or to be unveiled." In order to transform the earth into heaven, we must manifest or be unveiled, first to ourselves, and then to others. We are bona fide sons and daughters of God. The manifestation of our son/daughter-ship is so earthshaking that creation literally groans for this (Romans 8:16-22)!

THE AUTHENTIC YOU WAS MEANT TO BE UNVEILED FROM GLORY TO GLORY TO LOOK LIKE YOUR FLAVOR OF CHRIST.

That means the authentic you, who was created before the foundation of the world, was meant to be unveiled from glory to glory to look like your flavor of Christ. Second Corinthians 3:17-18 (New American Standard Bible) says,

Now the Lord is the Spirit, and where the Spirit of the Lord is, there

is liberty. But we all, with unveiled face, beholding as in a mirror the glory of the Lord, are being transformed into the same image from glory to glory, just as from the Lord, the Spirit.

And that glory is actually Christ in you (Colossians 1:27). Many, if not most of us, have had a hard time connecting experientially and emotionally with the truth of that. We are still stuck at some level of "yeah, but _____ is wrong with me." We are still having a struggle with our deficits, and this blocks us from seeing the fullness of why God sent us to the planet.

God, What Were You Thinking?

God, what were you thinking when you created me? Why was I put here on the planet? These are questions that have nagged each and every one of us on some level.

Often we give a nod to the idea that God created us for His pleasure. As good little Christians, we know we should give Him glory and worship Him. When I was a young believer, this constant praise and worship felt so impersonal – almost as if He created us as worshipping robots. It wasn't that I felt He wasn't worthy, I just felt He shouldn't have to be reminded all the time. Just being honest... Before I understood the beauty of this, I was frankly put off by the idea. I wondered, "Is God really so insecure that He constantly needs us to tell Him how great He is?" It really bugged me – kind of like the insecure woman who constantly needs to be told she is beautiful, because she does not really believe it in and of herself. Some of you may have wondered this too. It's OK, you are not a bad person.

When I finally searched out the whole praise and worship thing and brought it up to Him, I was amazed to find that He was not at all offended or surprised at my distaste. He actually thought the "why-should-I-constantly-praise-and-worship-You?" question was a great question. Talk about a secure God! AND He was so pleased to answer it!

God loves honest questions, even if they seem irreverent! He is authentic and not easily offended. He wants you to be authentic so He can minister the truth of Who He is for you right where you need it. Remember, Love is patient and Love is kind. Love is not easily offended (1 Corinthians 13:4-5). He wants you to know Him – the real Him! And He is pleased to answer your questions.

Sometimes when you don't get an answer, you might be asking the wrong question. Remember, in the vision, I asked Jesus if He was going to go with me into the molten gold lava river. He didn't answer me. The issue in my heart was really if I trusted Him enough that it was going to be OK. It wasn't until I flat out asked Him if it was going to be OK, that He answered me with a riveting, "You know Me." It was then I knew it was going to be OK, even if a lava dip was not in my grid of OK.

Sometimes He answers your questions with a question. We see God operating this way throughout scripture (Genesis 32:39; Judges 13:17-19; Matthew 19:17). Have you ever wondered why? God always wants to bring out the real issue on your heart. In my case, I was really wondering if I could trust God in the midst of a lava bath that did not make sense. He knew I knew Him enough to know I could. So all He had to do is remind me. Once I connected with the real issue, I could take the plunge. He is always after the deeper issues at hand, because He is always after our hearts. He knows us so much better than we have ever known ourselves. You can totally trust Him to know what you *really* need.

> ## NEITHER LOVE NOR SUBMISSION CAN BE DEMANDED AND STILL BE CALLED LOVE OR SUBMISSION...IT HAS TO BE FREELY GIVEN.

For those of you who have been secretly or not so secretly wondering what the deal is with the praise and worship, this might really help you. Of course He is worthy of all honor and praise. Perfection, holiness, power, and beauty inspire that. But Love doesn't demand it. The devil will pressure you for that. But neither love nor submission can be demanded and still be called love or submission. In order to be authentic love and authentic submission, it has to be freely given.

They are inside out choices made by the person they come from.

Love doesn't need your worship to fluff Him up, but you need to praise and worship Him and understand that He really is bigger than you. He is magnificent, kind, strong, wise, very present and helpful, and praise and worship are also the place where we can connect and commune in love. He is all about a full, satisfying, and, yes, even ecstatic love relationship. Here the oppression of the enemy slips off. Your perspective starts to align with His. The so-called big problems are strangely no big deal.

In this place, prayer is effective and effortless like breathing, because Love is present and faith works and is energized and made effective by Love.

Galatians 5:6 (AMPC) says,

> *For [if we are] in Christ Jesus, neither circumcision nor uncircumcision counts for anything, but only faith activated and energized and expressed and working through love.*

The circumcision or uncircumcision reference here can really be understood as the works we do to try to get closer or to please God. The stuff we do in our own strength and unbelief that God is really as good and present and powerful as He is, is exhausting. He never made us to toil. It is all about the work God has already done to get closer to his kids and the pleasure He has in His kids. We access all that through faith, which works when we are rooted and grounded in love. We will get back to this later.

God, What Were You Thinking About Me?

So it is clear that God created you and every other person for his pleasure and that we connect with Him in many ways, including our praise and worship, that flow naturally out of the place of encountering Him authentically.

When it comes to you, God is also not an existentialist nor a sadist; He is not a negligent Father, Who has so many kids He can only attend to His favorites. He doesn't have a random passing plan for you. You are here by design and for a very definite reason – with multiple reasons! You are not a cosmic accident.

God's word says,

> *But now [as things really are], God has placed and arranged the parts in the body, each one of them, just as He willed and saw fit [with the best balance of function]. (1 Corinthians 12:18 AMP)*

God has specific good things planned for you that He will reveal to you by His Spirit according to 1 Corinthians 2:9-12 (NIV):

> *"What no eye has seen, what no ear has heard, and what no human mind has conceived" – the things God has prepared for those who love him – these are the things God has revealed to us by his Spirit. The Spirit searches all things, even the deep things of God. For who knows a person's thoughts except their own spirit within them? In the same way, no one knows the thoughts of God except the Spirit of God. What we have received is not the spirit of the world, but the*

Spirit Who is from God, so that we may understand what God has freely given us.

Jeremiah 29:11 (NIV) says:

"For I know the plans I have for you," declares the Lord, "plans to prosper you and not to harm you, plans to give you hope and a future."

God not only designed you for very specific plans, but He also wants you to know them. As Schlyce Jimenez, my Apostle and close friend, says, "He gives you His phone number." Jeremiah 33:3 (AMP) puts it this way:

"Call to Me and I will answer you, and tell you [and even show you] great and mighty things, [things which have been confined and hidden], which you do not know and understand and cannot distinguish."

I like this verse so much, because it highlights where we get hung up. When it comes to specific plans for our lives, we perish for lack of knowledge (Hosea 4:6). We lack understanding and the ability to distinguish those great and mighty plans amidst all the noise in our lives. And what you cannot distinguish, you are overmastered by. Don't let the noise of life drown out the song in your heart!

God's answer: dial 33:3 – "Call Me." He wants you to know. But keep in mind, whatever you know, you have responsibility for. That is why He often reveals things step by step. We would simply freak out with the greatness of His plans for us and our intrinsic deficiencies to fulfill those. But we were never designed to fulfill anything apart from Him. Remember, apart from Him we can do nothing (John 15:5). We were made for dependence. We were made for ongoing, uninterrupted relationship (John 15:1-11).

GOD NOT ONLY DESIGNED YOU FOR VERY SPECIFIC PLANS, BUT HE ALSO WANTS YOU TO KNOW THEM.

What you need is unlocked and unveiled as you step out in faith and as you continue.

With that in mind, God not only has plans He reveals bit by bit, but He also has prearranged and made ready everything you would need to fulfill those plans (Ephesians 2:10 AMP):

> *For we are His workmanship [His own master work, a work of art], created in Christ Jesus [reborn from above – spiritually transformed, renewed, ready to be used] for good works, which God prepared [for us] beforehand [taking paths which He set], so that we would walk in them [living the good life which He prearranged and made ready for us].*

When Peter had to walk on the water, Jesus didn't suddenly make the water solid for Peter to step out upon. Peter had to step out, and Jesus provided the solid support of His Word for Peter to walk upon.

If we had everything in a tangible storehouse for our walk of faith, it wouldn't be a walk of faith. It would be going to the storehouse to grab what you already tangibly had. It would require no faith (Hebrews 11:1). It would require no dependency. It would require no relationship.

You have a definite purpose. Until you get more definition and direction about what that is, you will stumble around aimlessly and waste a lot of time and energy. Ask me how I know! When you do not know what the purpose of something is, abuse is inevitable.

DON'T LET THE NOISE OF LIFE DROWN OUT THE SONG IN YOUR HEART!

How many of you have a drawer full of bent forks because you used them to pry something – you get the picture.

When I decided at age seven I needed to do the hardest thing I could think of, I was trying to earn my sense of value from what I did. The hardest thing I could think of was to become a doctor. I didn't consult my own heart about what I had a passion for. I didn't consult God. I was driven by this need to prove I had value. The vow I made to become a doctor drove me for the next twenty years to fulfill that. However, by the time I did fulfill that, I realized there was a disconnect. My heart, as much as it was for my patients, was not engaged in practicing medicine. I finally had to connect with God, Who I had been running from. I had to, as Ephesians 2:10 says, get back on the path that God prepared for me beforehand, taking paths which He set, so that I could walk in it, living the good life which He prearranged and made ready for me.

For those of you who have been doing your own wandering or maybe out and out running away and feel you have missed your chance, let me encourage you. I was a really messed up but highly functioning twenty-seven-year-old by the time I quit going my own way and yielded to the God Who had been pursuing me my whole life. He can totally redeem the time. Joel 2:23-26 (AMPC) says,

> *Be glad then, you children of Zion, and rejoice in the Lord, your God; for He gives you the former or early rain in just measure and in righteousness, and He causes to come down for you the rain, the former rain and the latter rain, as before. And the [threshing] floors shall be full of grain and the vats shall overflow with juice [of the grape] and oil. And I will restore or replace for you the years that the locust has eaten – the hopping locust, the stripping locust, and the crawling locust, My great army which I sent among you. And you shall eat in plenty and be satisfied and praise the name of the Lord, your God, Who has dealt wondrously with you. And My people shall never be put to shame.*

WHAT YOU NEED IS UNLOCKED AND UNVEILED AS YOU STEP OUT IN FAITH AND AS YOU CONTINUE.

After I came to my senses, I had a lot of personal healing and mind renewal to do (more on that later). I had this terrible fear that I would miss it. If you are in that place, this scripture will give you a lot of comfort (Proverbs 19:21, NIV):

Many are the plans in a person's heart, but it is the Lord's purpose that prevails.

My translation: God is smarter than our stupid. Ask me how I know that. And I am so grateful for that!

My heart is aligned with God's heart in helping you connect with Love, connect with who you are in Love, connect with your purposes for Love, and be released and empowered with those purposes. It is a process of unveiling and discovery.

But recognize that as you discover your purpose, you will never truly fulfill that purpose by your own strength and striving. Remember what Jesus said, "Apart from me you can do no thing" (John 15:5).

The Anti-Kingdom Concept of Earning

GOD IS SMARTER THAN OUR STUPID.

Sons and daughters do not earn their place in the family. They are simply born into it by adoring parents who are looking to lavish inheritance on their kids, releasing it as they mature enough to handle it. Earning is not a kingdom concept. If we could earn it by even our most valiant efforts, it would be too cheap to reflect the goodness – the grace – of a God that defines and is the Source of all goodness.

Your place in the family is secure. There are no black sheep or forgotten members. Your identity as a beloved, highly-favored son or daughter has already been established. Love established it.

The language of earning and deserving is not the language of heaven. We get everything by inheritance.

Romans 8:14-17 (NIV) says,

YOUR PLACE IN THE FAMILY IS SECURE. LOVE ESTABLISHED IT.

For those who are led by the Spirit of God are the children of God. The Spirit you received does not make you slaves, so that you live in fear again; rather, the Spirit you received brought about your adoption to sonship. And by him we cry, "Abba, Father." The Spirit himself testifies with our spirit that we are God's children. Now if we are children, then we are heirs – heirs of God and co-heirs with Christ, if indeed we share in his sufferings in order that we may also share in his glory.

It never enters the minds of sons and daughters of good daddies to worry if they will get their needs or their heart desires fully met. They are a member of the household, and as such, have the privileges of the household. Servants earn wages, but sons and daughters are born into the privileges of the household. When they are old enough (read mature enough to handle it), they receive a full inheritance that they did not toil to earn.

The next time there is a "Did God say" when it comes to His promises to you, just shrug and say, "I don't know, go ask Him," and go on your merry, happy-go-lucky, carefree way!

You're an intrinsically adored child of God in a family with no black sheep. You have nothing to prove. It's already been settled. And it's

THE LANGUAGE OF EARNING AND DESERVING IS NOT THE LANGUAGE OF HEAVEN. WE GET EVERYTHING BY INHERITANCE.

been settled by the only One Whose vote really counts. You don't need to be rude or cocky, except to cut off the enemy of your soul. You can be confident that you've been chosen by the only One, Who has exquisitely perfect taste. The word of God says,

> *Even as [in His love] He chose us [actually picked us out for Himself as His own] in Christ before the foundation of the world, that we should be holy (consecrated and set apart for Him) and blameless in His sight, even above reproach, before Him in love. (Ephesians 1:4 AMPC)*

He confounds those who are wise in their own eyes and feel deserving of the family riches based on their own efforts (1 Corinthians 1:27). Many of you, who have been walking with the Lord and standing for a promise for a while, have experienced what it is like when the same promise instantaneously materializes for someone who barely knows the Lord. If you are honest, you can probably relate to the "wait a minute" knee-jerk response that tends to happen, because it just does not "seem fair." But I encourage you – be totally pumped for them! You have not been forgotten. You will receive the same promise of God by inheritance and rest and by celebrating others' victories. You never "earn the promise" by your faith, by your works, or by your holiness.

YOU'RE AN INTRINSICALLY ADORED CHILD OF GOD IN A FAMILY WITH NO BLACK SHEEP. YOU HAVE NOTHING TO PROVE. IT'S ALREADY BEEN SETTLED.

Self-righteousness in any flavor always stinks. Be careful not to slip into it. The test of how you handle others receiving a blessing you have waited on for a long time will reveal what is really in your heart. Allow any jealousy or resentment to come up, and bring it before God to cleanse you of it. If it is there, He knows it anyway.

He wants you free, happy, and celebrating in the lavish homecoming of any "younger prodigal brothers," not ticked and resentful that you didn't get what you labored for. Luke 15:28-32 (NIV) says:

The older brother became angry and refused to go in. So his father went out and pleaded with him. But he answered his father, "Look! All these years I've been slaving for you and never disobeyed your orders. Yet you never gave me even a young goat so I could celebrate with my friends. But when this son of yours who has squandered your property with prostitutes comes home, you kill the fattened calf for him!" "My son," the father said, "you are always with me, and everything I have is yours. But we had to celebrate and be glad, because this brother of yours was dead and is alive again; he was lost and is found."

See how Pappa pleads with us to be thrilled for others when they are blessed and do not deserve it? How it must have broken His heart to be accused of holding out on the older brother, who always already had everything! Both sons had already received their inheritance. The wayward son squandered his, and the older brother thought he was a servant and did not see that the entire time he had inherited the whole family farm to enjoy.

SELF-RIGHTEOUSNESS IN ANY FLAVOR ALWAYS STINKS.

When we see ourselves as servants and orphans, we misunderstand or flat out accuse the heart of God.

There is a classic musical called *Auntie Mame*, where the main character constantly urges people to, "Live, live, live!" because "Life is a banquet and most poor suckers are starving to death!" God often speaks volumes through what we often think is "secular." Don't miss your banquet by resenting someone else's fried chicken dinner! You and your faith never earned a morsel. The beautiful thing is that, if you never earned the good things in Christ, you cannot lose them.

Your union with Christ and the inheritance from that was made complete by the championship of God alone. We can't mess it up except if we insist on sulking outside the party!

Love Encounter Break #6

Let's take a break to encounter Love and have Him unveil a "why-am-I-here?" specific to you.

Pappa, I agree with the one reading this right now for the grace to rest and receive from You! You made them in Love with specific reasons why You sent them to planet earth. This is a discovery process, and I thank You for unveiling another aspect of those whys in a word or words, thoughts, pictures, feelings, impressions, a knowing, or however else you want to manifest. I thank You that You are helping them receive the beauty and glory intrinsic to those whys.

Now let yourself relax and let Love speak in those words, thoughts, pictures, feelings, impressions, knowings, or other manifestations. Jot down anything you are getting, however small. You know the drill by now. If you need reminders, feel free to go back to previous Encounter Break instructions and helps.

If you need more space, grab or make a new journal.

Love's unveiling of the reasons I am on planet Earth:

_____

_____

_____

_____

If you are having a hard time connecting with this, let me pray:

> *Pappa, help this one forgive themselves for everywhere they have not felt they have acted in line with the assignments they have been given and for the reasons behind those assignments. If this is not the issue, what is the lie that this one is believing that makes it hard to believe the truth that the assignments and the reasons behind the assignments they are sensing are truly theirs? What is the truth you want them to know?*

The lie Love is revealing that I believe about my life assignments and the whys behind them:

_____

_____

_____

_____

The truth Love is giving me about my life assignments and the whys behind them:

_____

_____

_____

_____

_____

_____

_____

What's Our Job?

So if everything we receive in Christ is by inheritance, what is our job? Do we sit on the couch with a smile on our face, one hand eating potato chips and the other hand held out?

Jesus's disciples asked Him the very same question in John 6:28-29 (AMP):

> *Then they asked Him, "What are we to do, so that we may habitually be doing the works of God?" Jesus answered, "This is the work of God: that you believe [adhere to, trust in, rely on, and have faith] in the One whom He has sent."*

How good a job did Jesus do on that cross? Did He really provide *everything* we need pertaining to life and godliness (2 Peter 1:3)? Does He really provide *all* our needs according to His riches in glory (Philippians 4:19)? Does He give us richly *all* things to enjoy (1 Timothy 6:17)? Were we really healed by His stripes (1 Peter 2:24)? Can we really do *all* things through Christ Who strengthens us (Philippians 4:13)? Can we really do the same works and greater works than Christ on the earth (John 14:12)? The list goes on.

God is looking for *believing* believers! When we believe with childlike faith, God is unencumbered to be everything He wants and planned to be for us in our situations.

This is not a beat-up session for the areas where we have unbelief.

Condemnation is simply not allowed (Romans 8:1). It is simply diagnostic to where we are, so we can authentically cry out like the father of the demonized boy: "I believe, help my unbelief!" (Mark 9:24).

Remember, God is the author and the finisher of our faith (Hebrews 12:2). He gets to singlehandedly save us in every meaning of the word! And that is His joy. It was for the joy set before Him that Jesus endured the cross! Hebrews 12:2 (KJV) says,

> *Looking unto Jesus the author and finisher of our faith; who for the joy that was set before him endured the cross, despising the shame, and is set down at the right hand of the throne of God.*

WHEN WE BELIEVE WITH CHILDLIKE FAITH, GOD IS UNENCUMBERED TO BE EVERYTHING HE WANTS AND PLANNED TO BE FOR US IN OUR SITUATIONS.

To have simple, childlike faith that moves mountains, we need to keep our focus riveted on Jesus. He gets to do *all* the heavy lifting. I love the Classic Amplified Version of Matthew 11:29:

> *Take My yoke upon you and learn of Me, for I am gentle (meek) and humble (lowly) in heart, and you will find rest (relief and ease and refreshment and recreation and blessed quiet) for your souls.*

Wherever the breakdown is, "turf it to Jesus," the Author and Finisher of your faith! What does that mean? Let me give you a visual. "Turf" is commonly used in American English as the ground or territory that belongs to someone. When you "turf" something, you literally kick it onto someone else's turf. In this case, whatever your deal is that is obstructing your ability to enter the rest of God, you can drop kick it over to God's turf. You place it in His happy in-basket. He gets to handle it. He gets to do all the heavy lifting. Love intends for us to cast all our cares upon Him, because He loves us (1 Peter 5:7). That means you get to be the recipient of Love's help wherever you need it. Jesus Himself said in John 15:5 (AMP),

LOVE GETS TO SINGLEHANDEDLY SAVE US IN EVERY MEANING OF THE WORD!

I am the Vine; you are the branches. The one who remains in Me and I in him bears much fruit, for [otherwise] apart from Me [that is, cut off from vital union with Me] you can do nothing.

So wherever and whenever you are struggling to believe something God has told you directly or through His Spirit-highlighted Word that you know is for you, let Love help you. Even faith itself only counts when it is activated, energized, expressed, and working through Love (Galatians 5:6 AMPC). "Turf it to Jesus" and let Him do all the heavy lifting as you yoke up with Love (Matthew 11:28-29).

Jesus and you are one with Holy Spirit, Who is your Helper, so recognize that you are letting God be God and Love be Love when you depend on His help. I'm a big "Jesus Turfer," and I invite you to do the same. It is a wonderful carefree way to live, casting all your cares on Him, because He really does attentively and affectionately care for you (1 Peter 5:7)!

Jesus is so compassionate, because He is Love and knows what it is like to be where we struggle.

Hebrews 4:15-16 says in the King James Version:

WHEREVER THE BREAKDOWN IS, "TURF IT TO JESUS," THE AUTHOR AND FINISHER OF YOUR FAITH!

For we have not an high priest which cannot be touched with the feeling of our infirmities; but was in all points tempted like as we are, yet without sin. Let us therefore come boldly unto the throne of grace, that we may obtain mercy, and find grace to help in time of need.

Check it out and read it again: Pappa's throne is made up of grace. So when we cry out, "I believe, help my unbelief," guess Who is doing the helping? The Three-in-One, Who loved you and gave Themselves up for you! Your job is to believe, and God's job is to help you do your job! He takes on the heavy lifting.

How does He do that? He helps transform our thinking so that we think like He does, and that transforms us (Romans 12:2). There is nothing like an encounter with God to get you thinking right!

God is able to move when we believe and simply rest in Him.

Hebrews 11:6 in the King James Version says,

> But without faith it is impossible to please him: for he that cometh to God must believe that he is, and that he is a rewarder of them that diligently seek him.

YOUR JOB IS TO BELIEVE, AND GOD'S JOB IS TO HELP YOU DO YOUR JOB!

Faith pleases Him because He can manifest the goodness of His nature through the conduit of faith.

However, we still need to put our hands to the work in front of us. He is a Rewarder of those who diligently seek Him, and He will not reward laziness. He's a good Pappa and is raising champions, who operate out of rest and joy, not entitled loafers.

Our job must involve the ongoing renewal of our minds to the goodness of God, His promises and simple childlike faith that they will come to pass for us. We need to bathe in all that ridiculous, unearned, ongoing, and unending love, and look at our Creator, ourselves, and others through the eyes of Love. And, as I said earlier, love activates and energizes our faith and makes it effective (Galatians 5:6).

Getting our minds wrapped around Who Love is, who we are, and what is ours by inheritance is what is involved with scriptural mind renewal. It is here that we see transformation in ourselves, our lives, and the lives around us. We are urged not to be conformed to the patterns and mold of the world around us, but to be transformed by that mind renewal (Romans 12:2).

This sounds so easy, but we have to trust God to help us get there from here. We cannot simply jam truth into ourselves and call it mind renewal. As we encounter Love, we are automatically transformed in the renewal of our minds from glory to glory (Romans 12:2; 2 Corinthians 3:18). And Love is just the One to get us there from here as we look to Him.

Our only job is to believe and trust Him to help us get there from wherever messed up place we are at. And He will provide some way to renew our thinking so we can believe, despite our unbelief (Mark 9:24).

7.

GETTING THERE FROM HERE – FINISHING AT THE STARTING POINT

A Jesus Infomercial

One of my pet peeves is to read a book or hear someone talk and the majority of the time is spent on discussing a problem. Most of the time, if people are looking for answers, they already know they have a problem. But when you spend the majority of the time unpacking just how bad the problem really is, you go from having a problem to really being depressed about the problem. You thought it was bad, but you didn't think it was *that* bad! Yay, thanks!

One thing I love about God is that He started with the end in mind. The word of God says that Jesus was the Lamb slain before the foundation of the world (Revelation 13:8). Talk about proactive! The Trinity had the solution all wrapped up in the person of Christ before there ever was a problem! I wonder what a Jesus infomercial would be like. "Here's the Solution. I've already purchased it for you! You just need to believe that it's in your bank account, and I'll help you do even that. And, oh yeah, here are all the problems it covers!" BAM!

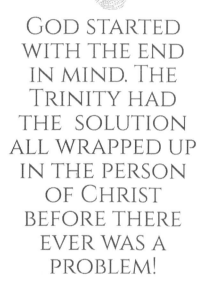

GOD STARTED WITH THE END IN MIND. THE TRINITY HAD THE SOLUTION ALL WRAPPED UP IN THE PERSON OF CHRIST BEFORE THERE EVER WAS A PROBLEM!

What a deal! I'm so glad I'm signed up!

Only God is that masterful and that good! Kind of makes satan look like an idiot.

But I know we live in real time. You've got stuff – big stuff, small stuff, and every size in between. Your stuff seems real and heavy and big and loud. Your stuff hurts.

Enter Jesus. He gets your stuff. He gets you with your stuff. He feels your stuff!

Hebrews 4:15 says in the King James Version:

> *For we have not an high priest which cannot be touched with the feeling of our infirmities; but was in all points tempted like as we are, yet without sin.*

Jesus is God with flesh on. On the earth He sweated and stank (think Middle East, no indoor plumbing and no deodorant). He had normal bodily functions. He was around really annoying dense people as his closest companions! Cases in point:

> *Whenever it seizes him, it throws him to the ground. He foams at the mouth, gnashes his teeth, and becomes rigid. I asked your disciples to drive out the spirit, but they could not. "You unbelieving generation," Jesus replied, "how long shall I stay with you? How long shall I put up with you? Bring the boy to me." (Mark 9:18-19 NIV)*

Peter said,

> *"Explain the parable to us."*
> *"Are you still so dull?" Jesus asked them. (Matthew 15:15-16 NIV)*

I don't know. I may need to repent, but it just makes me feel better! Jesus got annoyed! His annoyance did not negate His wild love for His disciples. Jesus did not sin. He did not violate love, but He still was annoyed. How human! So Love gets what it is like to live, sweat, struggle, get tired, be tempted, feel pain, get falsely accused, get attacked, and so on and so on. Whatever you are dealing with, Love intimately gets it!

All Things

So when Jesus died on the cross and said, "It is finished" (John 19:30), it was actually something that was mystically finished before the world even had a foundation. God has it so covered that the problems start to look like a joke.

That is not to say that the suffering you feel is a joke. God is serious about your heart, and He's serious about your pain. He just looks at the cause as a joke – because compared to Him, it is. He is seriously confident that the big-A Answer came before the little-p problem.

WHATEVER YOU ARE DEALING WITH, LOVE INTIMATELY GETS IT!

Love swallowed all of it up in Himself. He is, in fact, drawing all things to Himself. That is why:

- You can do **all things** through Him, Who provides the strength (Philippians 4:13). **All things** are possible with Him (Matthew 19:26; Mark 10:27).
- **All things** work together for our good (Romans 8:28).
- In seeking the Kingdom first, **all things** will be added (Matthew 6:33).
- **All things** have been committed to Jesus by Pappa (Matthew 11:27; Luke 10:22).

- Through him **all things** were made; without Him nothing was made that has been made (John 1:3).
- Pappa put **all things** under His power (John 13:13).
- Holy Spirit will teach us **all things** and will remind us of everything Jesus has said (John 14:26; 1 John 2:27).
- His hand has made **all things** (Isaiah 66:1, 2).

Pappa, Who did not spare His own Son, but gave Him up for us all – how will He not also, along with Him, graciously give us all things (Romans 8:32)?

For from Him and through Him and for Him are all things (Romans 11:36). The Spirit searches all things, even the deep things of God (1 Corinthians 2:10).

> WHATEVER YOUR DEAL IS, LOVE IS SERIOUSLY CONFIDENT THAT THE BIG-A ANSWER CAME BEFORE THE LITTLE-P PROBLEM.

Pappa is where all things came from and for Whom we live; and Jesus Christ, through Whom all things came and through Whom we live (1 Corinthians 8:6).

He is able to bless us abundantly, so that in all things at all times, having all that we need, we will abound in every good work (2 Corinthians 9:8).

He made known to us the mystery of His will according to His good pleasure, which He purposed in Christ, to bring unity to all things in heaven and on earth under Christ (Ephesians 1:9-11).

Pappa placed all things under Jesus's feet and appointed Jesus to be head over everything for the church (Ephesians 1:22).

He has made known the mystery of the boundless riches of Christ, Who created all things (Ephesians 3:8-9).

I also want to quote this "mother" of all scriptures straight up. Check this out:

> *For in him all things were created: things in heaven and on earth, visible and invisible, whether thrones or powers or rulers or authorities; all things have been created through him and for him. He is before all things, and in him all things hold together. And he is the head of the body, the church; he is the beginning and the firstborn from among the dead, so that in everything he might have the supremacy. For God was pleased to have all his fullness dwell in him, and through him to reconcile to himself all things, whether things on earth or things in heaven, by making peace through his blood, shed on the cross. (Colossians 1:16-20 NIV)*

God's Final word was His Son.

> *He has spoken to us by His Son, Whom He appointed heir of all things, and through Whom also He made the universe. The Son is the radiance of God's glory and the exact representation of His being, sustaining all things by His powerful word. (Hebrews 1:2-3 NIV)*

And finally in the book of Revelation to cap it all off:

"He is worthy to receive glory and honor and power, for He created all things, and by His will they were created and have their being." (Revelation 4:11)

I think we can agree: God had us covered in *all things*! We can afford to relax.

LOVE HAD US COVERED IN ALL THINGS! WE CAN AFFORD TO RELAX.

I put these verses in Appendix A so you can find them easily when you feel stressed or overwhelmed, and need to be reminded that you and your loved ones and situation are covered!

Love Encounter Break #7

Let's take a break to encounter Love and have Him reveal how masterfully Love has you and all the details of your life completely and masterfully covered.

Pappa, I agree with the one reading this right now for the grace to rest and receive from You! You made them in Love and have covered them with Your love in every area. I thank You for revealing what that looks like specifically for them in a word or words, thoughts, pictures, feelings, impressions, a knowing, or however else you want to manifest. I thank You that You are helping them receive You and your covering for themselves and all the details of their life.

Now let yourself relax and let Love speak in those words, thoughts, pictures, feelings, impressions, knowings, or other manifestations.

Jot down anything you are getting, however small. If you need more space, grab or make a new journal.

Love's unveiling of how He covers you and the details of your life:

_____

_____

_____

_____

_____

_____

If you are having a hard time connecting with this, let me pray:

Pappa, if there were people who did not cover or protect this son or daughter or who neglected them or abused them in some other way, please let them know and give them the grace so they can release them in forgiveness. If there was a situation where they felt You did not cover them, please bring this in their consciousness and give them the grace so they can forgive You. (When God brings up these people, release them in forgiveness.)

If this is not the issue, what is the lie that this one is believing that makes it hard for them to believe the truth that they and the details of their life are intimately and totally covered? What is the truth You want them to know?

The lie Love is revealing that I believe about God not covering me or the details of my life:

_____

_____

_____

_____

The truth Love is giving me about God truly covering me and the details of my life:

_____

_____

_____

_____

A Relaxed God

One characteristic that has surprised and thrilled me over and over in my encounters with God is that He is *so relaxed*! I may not be relaxed about my situation, but He is. He is infinitely confident in Himself to resolve all the things that we find so big. He is so much bigger than anything we are facing.

This brings to mind another vision I had with Jesus. Again, we were in hell (yeah, I know, but Jesus never asked for my input regarding my encounter preferences). We were walking through a maze of trails in hell, that were so overwhelmingly complex and intricate, I knew I'd never get out without Him. As we were walking, there were demons lining the sides and the walls, and they were trying to taunt and intimidate me, with the aim of tormenting and overwhelming me. When I lagged behind Jesus, I could feel them increasingly overwhelm me so that hell felt so real and the particles of my very being wanted to explode. The closest thing that I can relate it to is the famous haunting painting by Edvard Munch titled *The Scream*. But when I, with all my particles of being, caught up to Jesus, I was totally fine. In fact, I was so good that I began to taunt the demons: "You want a piece of ME?" And they were freaking out in torment.

The take-home lesson: when all hell comes against you, stick close to Jesus! Sounds scriptural, huh?

Hebrews 12:2 (KJV) says:

Wherefore seeing we also are compassed about with so great a cloud of witnesses, let us lay aside every weight, and the sin which doth so easily beset us, and let us run with patience the race that is set before us, looking unto Jesus the author and finisher of our faith; who for the joy that was set before him endured the cross, despising the shame, and is set down at the right hand of the throne of God.

Another fascinating thing about Jesus in this vision as I observed Him, was His *focus*. He was totally unconcerned about the stupid demons all around. He was on a mission, with His face set like flint, but relaxed on His mission to lead me out of hell.

But He also was not at all in a hurry to get me out of there – an irksome fact that did not escape me. We were going to trek through hell until I got the revelation that I was born to be not only totally good, but also in total authority in the midst of the den of the enemy – as long as I was sticking close to Him.

Christ is relaxed in His total supremacy. He has total confidence in Who He is and what He has done. He's got this! And He's got us!

The problem is that we tend to forget. There is no condemnation in Christ Jesus for forgetting, but when we do, darkness can overwhelm us. There is no fear in love. But there is torment when we are separated from Love in our minds.

That is why it is not optional to walk in His Spirit (Romans 8:1, 4, 14) and take every thought captive to obedience (2 Corinthians

10:4-5). It is not optional to be transformed by the renewing of our minds and to agree with Who He is and what He has done for us and who we are (Romans 12:2).

OK, great! But lest you take on the burden of another project in your own strength, remember: apart from Him you can do nothing!!! This is not yours to do alone! As a matter a fact, smarty-pants, you can't do this alone.

And that makes a great segue into our next chapter!

8.

FREAKY REST

The Strength of Love

Okay, let's agree Love is nice, in the truest, most non-obnoxious, most non-namby-pamby sense of the word.

But Love has called us to do some hefty things. Actually, He has called us to do impossible things. He does this because we are called to be sons and daughters, and look and act like sons and daughters. He is the God Who makes all things are possible. He lords over the impossible. And He expects us to co-rule and co-reign over the impossible. What a job description!

But this is only possible because He did the most consummate of hefty things. He has leveled the playing field. The mountains have been brought low, and the valleys have been raised up (Isaiah 40:4; 49:11).

Like modern balladeers sing, Love truly is the answer. And Love never fails (1 Corinthians 13:8). He has swallowed everything up into Himself. And, unlike what the twenty-four-hour news stations tout (and like much of the Church, obsessing on freaky end-times doctrines), His kingdom is manifesting at a *phenomenal* rate!

And it is accelerating, so much so that the universe is struggling to keep pace, expanding to fulfill everything all in all with Him and His benevolent kingdom in manifestation. And He has chosen to release and unveil His kingdom through His kids. No wonder, our heavenly identities need to manifest!

LOVE LORDS OVER THE IMPOSSIBLE.

Holy Goo, Batman!

Even the earth is groaning for us as sons and daughters to be unveiled with our truest selves (Romans 8:19-23). And we can all (hopefully) agree that we have a ways to go. If any of us think we have arrived, one has to wonder if the destination was really worth getting to! As great as our accomplishments may be, there is always more. The joy is in the journey!

But it is not about self-improvement or changing ourselves. I remember for years I would exhaust myself with the latest self-improvement program. I was on my own program-of-the-month club, because I saw so many, many things that needed changing! Holy Spirit was patiently waiting for me to eject my own self-improvement program. He had to wait quite a while until I totally exhausted myself. Maybe that is you. If it is, then my heart and really good advice for you are to just to chuck your self-improvement calisthenics. Give it up already!

> LOVE HAS SWALLOWED EVERYTHING UP INTO HIMSELF. AND HE HAS CHOSEN TO RELEASE AND UNVEIL HIS KINGDOM THROUGH HIS KIDS.

We are called to go from glory to glory. But never forget this is a *supernatural* process. It is a process of being unveiled to line up with your authentic self.

The word of God says in Philippians 2:13 (I like the Amplified Classic Version best):

[Not in your own strength] for it is God Who is all the while effectually at work in you [energizing and creating in you the power and desire], both to will and to work for His good pleasure and satisfaction and delight.

•Point #1 It is not in your own strength – it is in the strength of Love. And Love never fails, by the way (1 Corinthians 13:8).

•Point #2 Holy Spirit is continually at work transforming you. The caveat is He often works in places you wouldn't have chosen. Guess who is smarter than you?

•Point #3 He is really good at His job.

•Point #4 If you are not thrilled with the process, He can give you the energy to cooperate. Thank You, Holy Spirit!

•Point #5 He can also give you the "want to." Sometimes, you are not really willing, but you can be willing to let God make you willing. Or, if you are such a super hard case, you can be willing to be willing to be willing. Ask me how I know.

•Point #6 Even though He is the Source, there is work you need to do – often it is to quit fighting God in the process He is doing. It reminds me of the child who is hitting you as you are trying to look at and minister to the "boo-boo."

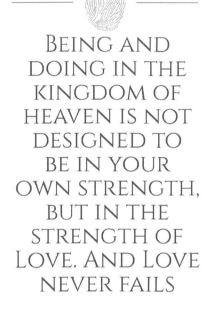

BEING AND DOING IN THE KINGDOM OF HEAVEN IS NOT DESIGNED TO BE IN YOUR OWN STRENGTH, BUT IN THE STRENGTH OF LOVE. AND LOVE NEVER FAILS

•Point #7 It is about His good pleasure, satisfaction, and delight. Now as you mature in delighting in God in all your ways, He will give you the desires of your heart (Psalm 37:4). It is easy to delight in Love. I LOVE this verse! It has helped me so very much!

We truly need to be transformed; our form needs to be transferred experientially to another kingdom. Our form literally needs to be taken out of agreement with the kingdom of darkness and fear, "on, to and in with agreement with the other side," which is the Kingdom of Light and Love.

The word of God says we literally have been translated there and we

LOVE IS CONTINUALLY AT WORK TRANSFORMING YOU.

are of that Kingdom (Colossians 1:13). The challenge is that we don't know it, we don't recognize it, we have forgotten it, or we are not choosing accordingly. But Love is there to help! Remember that renewing your mind thing? We just can't get away from it. And Love won't let us.

The word *transform* is from the Greek word *metamorphóō* which means "to change into another form," "to metamorphose," or "to transfigure." The illustration God gave us, in living unfolding color, is a lowly, seemingly insignificant caterpillar metamorphosing into a beautiful, free, inspiring butterfly.

Think about it. The caterpillar is no astrophysicist. It instinctively knows there is a time to cocoon – separate and insulate themselves from the world. As it does that, the inner process unfolds automatically. The caterpillar is doing nothing. I understand it basically turns into goo as it is reformed in the cocoon.

How many of you have felt the intense discomfort of having no control in the process of being melted into goo as the Lord is working His transformation process in you? I can relate!

It helps a lot if you are aware of the process that He is doing, so you can relax and quit fighting Him in it. If you are feeling that weird uncomfortable feeling, you might want to ask Holy Spirit, "What are You working in me?" Really, He is always up to something. You can set-

TRUST LOVE TO HELP YOU STAY AWAKE TO THE TRUTH THAT YOU HAVE BEEN TRANSLATED OUT OF THE KINGDOM OF DARKNESS INTO THE KINGDOM OF LIGHT!

tle down and cooperate when you know that God is good and is up to something good. Even if it is painful right now, it is temporary, and the results will be amazing and worth it. Knowing this and allowing it will help you get through and get through quicker. Can I hear an amen!

If He is working patience in you, it will be a season of the most annoying exasperating snafus, people, holdups, and prolonged standing on the promises. But let me help you. The fastest way is through – just buck it up and let Him do it! I tell people over and over, if you are going to suffer (and there is no way around this), make sure to get a really big bang for your buck!

On the other side is something breathtaking – an upgraded version more in line with the real you! You have just been promoted to another level of glory (2 Corinthians 3:18). You are looking more like Love all the time! You are being conformed into the image of Christ. That, in fact, is your destiny (Romans 8:29).

You were marked by Love to make your mark of love!

BEING CONFORMED TO THE IMAGE OF CHRIST IS NOT COMFORTABLE, BUT ON THE OTHER SIDE IS SOMETHING BREATHTAKING, AN UPGRADED VERSION OF YOU!

Putting on Your Depends

We all do need to manifest and manifest with all the fruit of the Spirit. Let's check out this tall order. The famous Sunday-school felt-board illustration verse is Galatians 5:22-23. And guess what, we never out grew it. It says (NASB),

But the fruit of the Spirit is love, joy, peace, patience, kindness, goodness, faithfulness, gentleness, self-control; against such things there is no law.

Love itself is defined by 1 Corinthians 13:4-8 (AMPC):

Love endures long and is patient and kind; love never is envious nor

boils over with jealousy, is not boastful or vainglorious, does not display itself haughtily. It is not conceited (arrogant and inflated with pride); it is not rude (unmannerly) and does not act unbecomingly. Love (God's love in us) does not insist on its own rights or its own way, for it is not self-seeking; it is not touchy or fretful or resentful; it takes no account of the evil done to it [it pays no attention to a suffered wrong].It does not rejoice at injustice and unrighteousness but rejoices when right and truth prevail. Love bears up under anything and everything that comes, is ever ready to believe the best of every person, its hopes are fadeless under all circumstances, and it endures everything [without weakening]. Love never fails [never fades out or becomes obsolete or comes to an end].

Anyone exhausted yet? Exactly! If you could do it in your own strength, superman/woman, you wouldn't need God. He created us for dependency! Yup! The great American independent spirit needs to bite the dust! The Marlboro Man already died of cancer. Let it go! It is time to put on your "depends" and be happy about it! Jesus always does the heavy lifting, but you have to let Him.

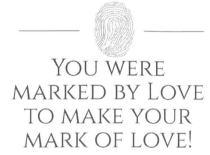

YOU WERE MARKED BY LOVE TO MAKE YOUR MARK OF LOVE!

Matthew 11:28-30 (AMPC) says so beautifully (if you will actually read and savor it – hint, hint):

Come to Me, all you who labor and are heavy-laden and overburdened, and I will cause you to rest. [I will ease and relieve and refresh your souls.] Take My yoke upon you and learn of Me, for I am gentle (meek) and humble (lowly) in heart, and you will find rest (relief and ease and refreshment and recreation and blessed quiet) for your souls. For My yoke is wholesome (useful, good not harsh, hard, sharp, or pressing, but comfortable, gracious, and pleasant), and My burden is light and easy to be borne.

IF YOU COULD DO IT IN YOUR OWN STRENGTH, YOU WOULDN'T NEED GOD. HE CREATED YOU FOR DEPENDENCY. LET LOVE DO THE HEAVY LIFTING!

How do "ease, relief, refreshment, recreation and blessed quiet for your souls" grab you? Jesus always fits. He is not harsh, hard, sharp, or pressing, but comfortable, gracious, pleasant, and light!

If you are going to make the love mark that Love marked you to make, you are going to have to depend on Love. He will make the assignment fit you and make you fit for the assignment. He will make the journey worthwhile. Love will make the impossible, possible.

What the Heck Is Abiding?

Fruit never squeezes itself out. It is the result of hanging out on the tree, vine, or bush. It is just programmed to pop out, and if it does not, something is wrong.

Well the "fruit of us" and what is in us is designed to pop out, and if it does not, something is wrong. There has been a "disconnect."

Jesus had a lot to say about this. John 15:1, 4-8 (AMP) says:

> *I am the true Vine, and My Father is the vinedresser. Remain in Me, and I [will remain] in you. Just as no branch can bear fruit by itself without remaining in the vine, neither can you [bear fruit, producing evidence of your faith] unless you remain in Me. I am the Vine; you are the branches. The one who remains in Me and I in him bears much fruit, for [otherwise] apart from Me [that is, cut off from vital union with Me] you can do nothing. If anyone does not remain in Me, he is thrown out like a [broken off] branch, and withers and dies; and they gather such branches and throw them into the fire, and they are burned. If you remain in Me and My words remain in you [that is, if we are vitally united and My message lives in your heart], ask whatever you wish and it will be done for you. My Father is glorified and honored by this, when you bear much fruit, and prove yourselves to be My [true] disciples.*

LOVE MAKES THE IMPOSSIBLE, POSSIBLE.

Jesus makes it really clear. We need to abide in Him. Our fruit comes from remaining or abiding in Him. The word abide is really an old-fashioned word, but it is worth "bringing back." It is rich! According to Merriam-Webster Online Dictionary, abide means:

- To "wait for,"
- to "endure without yielding,"

- to "withstand,"
- to "bear patiently,"
- to "accept without objection,"
- to "tolerate,"
- to "remain stable," and most importantly,
- to "continue in a place."

We need to continue to stay connected to Jesus – to literally stay in Love, and the fruit and exploits will pop out, eventually.

We use the term "in love" for the emotional euphoria we feel when we are totally smitten with someone, especially when they love us back. However, here I am referring to abiding in God as Love. Practically, that means we are staying consciously connected to God regularly and on an ongoing basis. This is practicing a consciousness of His Presence, talking to Him about the ongoing details of your day, listening to Him with spiritual ears, seeing Him with spiritual eyes, enjoying just hanging out, asking Him questions, and listening for the answers just like you would your best friend or spouse. And He cares about all the details!

The word of God says that we can practice and train our spiritual senses to discern good and evil (Hebrews 5:14).

Reading God's word is paramount because it is the standard by which Truth is revealed. Other excellent spiritual disciplines will also help you hone your spiritual senses. These include memorizing God's Word, pondering (or meditating) on God's word, praying, worshipping, fasting, hearing and obeying, praising, listening to godly preaching and teaching, reading good books (shameless plug), sharing and listening to testimonies of how God has moved, journaling, ministering to the sick, and the list goes on.

LOVE'S PRESENCE IS ALWAYS RIGHT WHERE YOU ARE. PRACTICE DISCERNING IT.

Love's Presence is always right where you are. It takes discernment to connect with Him, which you get better and better at by practicing.

All the Love Encounters in this book are actually training your senses to connect with God and stay experientially connected with God. As you apply yourself in rest, you typically should be finding it easier and easier to connect with God. If a particular section is more difficult, most likely it involves an area where you are more strongly bound up. Pushing through can get you past that. But do not be ashamed to get help if you need it.

So abiding in God brings automatic fruitfulness. As we are rooted and grounded in Love, which is a supernaturally empowered process, the word of God says that we "may be filled to the measure of all the fullness of God" (Ephesians 3:16-19). Now that's what I call bearing fruit!

Interestingly, all this abiding and being fruitful in the book of John is in the context of Love. Check this out.

ABIDING IN LOVE BRINGS AUTOMATIC GORGEOUS FRUIT.

John 15:9-11 (AMP) goes on to say,

I have loved you just as the Father has loved Me; remain in My love [and do not doubt My love for you]. If you keep My commandments and obey My teaching, you will remain in My love, just as I have kept My Father's commandments and remain in His love. I have told you these things so that My joy and delight may be in you, and that your joy may be made full and complete and overflowing.

We are called to camp out – abide in Love!

Laboring to Rest – Seriously?

We are called to rest in Christ. Hebrews 4:1, 3, 5, 9-11 (Voice) says,

That's why, as long as that promise of entering God's rest remains open to us, we should be careful that none of us seem to fall short ourselves. We who believe are entering into salvation's rest even though God's works were finished from the very creation of the world. There is much discussion of "rest" in what we are calling the First Testament of Scripture. God rests on the seventh day after creation. In the Ten Commandments, God commands His people to remember the Sabbath day, keep it holy, and do no work. By letting go of daily work, they declared their absolute dependence on God to meet their needs. We do not live by the work of our hands, but by the bread and word that God supplies. But a greater rest is yet to come when we will be released from all suffering, and when we will inherit the earth. Jesus embodies this greater rest that still awaits the people of God, a people fashioned through obedience and faith. If some of us fail to enter that rest, it is because we fail to answer the call. There still remains a place of rest, a true Sabbath, for the people of God because those who enter into salvation's rest lay down their labors in the same way that God entered into a Sabbath rest from His. So let us move forward to enter this rest, so that none of us fall into the kind of faithless disobedience that prevented them from entering.

In this translation, it says rather mildly to "move forward" to enter His rest.

ALLOW LOVE TO FILL YOU TO THE MEASURE OF ALL HIS FULLNESS.

Other translations say:

- "labor" (KJV)
- "be diligent" (NASB)
- "make every effort" (NIV)
- "keep at it and eventually arrive at the place of rest" (Message)
- "do our best" (CJB)

The funniest and most "in-your-face" one is the Amplified Classic Version: "be zealous and exert ourselves and strive diligently."

I remember reading that and thinking, "Seriously, God? What does *that* look like?" It looks like, you guessed it, mind renewal. It takes labor, zealousness, and exertion to take thoughts captive.

That labor looks something like this: "Hey, thought, you are not a 'God thought.' You are exalting yourself against Who God is. I will choose to think thoughts in line with Who God is, who He says I am, who He says others are, and what He says about my situation."

When you get pain or cancer or something else wrong in your body, who gets to be the boss in your mind? Do the symptoms and doctors' diagnoses get to be the final authority? Or does the One, by whose stripes you were healed (1 Peter 2:24), get to be Lord? You choose. The pressure will be for your heart and your mind, and hence your words, to line up with the natural circumstances and any demonic overlay versus what God has said. Out of the abundance of the heart the mouth speaks (Matthew 12:24). As you hang out with Love – His fruit, His faith, His peace, His promises – He will come out in abundance!

IN YOUR SITUATION, WHO WILL YOU LET BE LORD – THE PROBLEM, OR THE ONE WHO OVER-MASTERED IT? LET LOVE HELP YOU DECIDE.

Faith is rest. Your labor is to get in faith and stay in faith – to get in rest and to stay in rest. And it is a real battle at times. You will have to look unto Jesus, the author and the finisher or perfecter of your faith (Hebrews 12:2).

I remember when my youngest daughter was around three. My husband was on prolonged deployment in the navy, and I was getting her into her jammies. When I pulled down her un-

AS YOU HANG OUT WITH LOVE – HIS FRUIT, HIS FAITH, HIS PEACE, HIS PROMISES – HE WILL COME OUT IN ABUNDANCE!

derwear, there was bright red blood, and not just a little. Being a physician, I knew that what doctors call the "differential" (potential causes) was not good: physical/sexual trauma, a benign adrenal tumor involving major surgery, or localized cancer. As a mom who had a background of sexual abuse as a child, the freak out was off the charts. And, of course, my husband was unreachable and thousands of miles away. A spirit of fear grabbed me by the throat, and all I could do was pray in the Spirit. I knew the *next thing* to come out of my mouth was how this deal was going to go. So I continued to pray in the Spirit as I called the doctor. My daughter's pediatrician, by her tone, was clearly thinking "hysterical mother," but told me to bring her in. As I continued to pray, faith started to arise (and I knew it wasn't my measly faith). Holy Spirit brought just the right scriptures to speak over my daughter. By the time I got to the office, I was in my right mind, still somewhat anxious, but not under the attack. The doctor took one look at her underwear and said, "No, I don't have to test this." It was clearly blood (I felt vindicated). Her examination revealed neither trauma nor cancerous growth. We did an ultrasound, which revealed only normal adrenals. There was, in fact, no medical explanation at all. She was diagnosed with "idiopathic vaginal bleeding." *Idiopathic* is the medical term for "we have no clue, but we still want to sound professional." Imagine that! Spiritual attacks with physical manifestations are not in the medical community's differential of potential causes for things, but it should be in yours. Stay alert and steady, but not fearful or paranoid. Holy Spirit will lead you. You were BORN to rule over this!

How did the story end? We decided just to watch how things went. I was not going to subject my sweet little girl to any more testing, and to this day she thankfully doesn't remember the episode. The bleeding disappeared and mysteriously never returned (except on schedule). But it really was no mystery. I let Jesus be Lord over my heart and mouth as I reigned in those emotions and let Him stir up the

FAITH IS REST. LET LOVE HELP YOU GET THERE AND STAY THERE.

faith that was needed, and He took care of the His daughter's problem. Thank You, Jesus! My job as a daughter was not to toil over scripture to eke out a healing. My job was to labor to enter His rest and let Love be God. And in this case it was war. But we won! His Word says apart from Him we can do *no thing* (John 15:5). It takes

His grace to renew our minds. It takes grace to enter and stay in rest in the areas where our minds are in a battle.

No amount of Bible study, prayer, confession, prophetic decrees, fasting, deliverance, teaching, impartation, counseling, or mental calisthenics, apart from Him, will do anything but cause frustration, disillusionment, and flat-out exhaustion. Ask me how I know that. Coming to the end of yourself really sucks, but it is exactly the place where Love steps in and shows off!

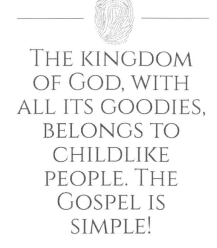

THE KINGDOM OF GOD, WITH ALL ITS GOODIES, BELONGS TO CHILDLIKE PEOPLE. THE GOSPEL IS SIMPLE!

Love is thrilled to help in the labor to enter rest, where you are simply having childlike faith. Remember the kingdom of God, with all its goodies, belongs to childlike people (Matthew 18:3). Well-loved and cared for children do not toil. When we give up toiling is when God gets to be God, and He is really good at His job!

You have been marked by Love to do exploits – let Him be amazing through you!

— *Love Encounter Break #8* —

Let's take a break to encounter Love and have Him reveal the areas in which you struggle to rest.

Pappa, I agree with the one reading this right now for the grace to rest and receive from You – especially in the area of rest! You made them in Love and made them to rest even while going about doing the assignments You have for them and during the storms they encounter. I thank You for revealing what that looks like specifically for them in a word or words, thoughts, pictures, feelings, impressions, a knowing, or however else you want to manifest. I thank you that You are helping them to rest while they are grappling with the things that try to take them out of rest.

Now let yourself relax and let Love speak in those words, thoughts, pictures, feelings, impressions, knowings, or other manifestations.

Jot down anything you are getting, however small. If you need more space, grab or make a new journal.

Love's unveiling of the areas that you struggle to rest and be at peace with:

_____

_____

_____

_____

What are the lies that you are believing about these areas?

_____

_____

_____

_____

_____

What are the truths Love is giving you about those areas, to empower you to get into rest and to stay in rest as He works out things for good?

_____

_____

_____

_____

_____

_____

_____

_____

9.
TRUE
CONFESSIONS

Early Years

The circumstances surrounding my birth were supernatural. I was born three months premature in a tiny community hospital in Vermont. There weren't any NICUs back then, and little to support my fight to live. But fight I did, as I was told by my grandmother, who said I would kick and kick and kick. I was not expected to live, and if I did, there was real concern about my neurological development (i.e., brain damage). Because my stay in the hospital was so long and the staff was not sure I was going to be "normal," both a nurse and the doctor offered to adopt me if my parents did not feel they could care for me (wow – right?). The nurse, in fact, visited me about twelve years later and was floored that I was healthy and developing normally. Someone must have been praying. *Love had marked me with the miraculous.*

I do believe, though, that at some point I must have died or visited heaven. I remember at a very early age (around two or three) feeling desperate that I was "forgetting the way to heaven" and I needed to remember. I could feel that knowledge slipping away. *Love had marked me with a consciousness and a connection to heaven.*

I had powerful encounters with the Lord before I could even remember much of anything else as a child. Jesus would appear at various times, especially when I was in emotional pain, and I knew He loved me and I loved Him. *Love had marked me with the experience of comfort, His Presence, and unconditional supernatural love.*

But I didn't know His name or His Gospel of grace and love. I did not know that this Man was the way that I was desperately trying not to forget. I would have dreams of going down paths to find and climb a long ladder to heaven. I would dive into a huge deep blue pool of bliss. I didn't realize this Man was The Way and He was The Ladder, and His Spirit was the Pool. *Love had marked me with the bliss of heaven.*

I remember Him visiting me when I was five in kindergarten in a field of wildflowers and butterflies when I was in emotional pain because a little girl had attacked me, out of the blue. I just couldn't figure out why she hated me so much. He was there to comfort me. *Love had marked me with the reality of encountering Love and freedom.*

My family traveled across Europe, and I kept seeing this Man hanging on a cross over the bed headboards. No one explained this to me, and I didn't understand the cross, but I knew this was the Man I had met and that I loved Him because He loved me. *Love had marked me with the Gospel, without words.*

I loved to go to my friends' churches – Catholic or Protestant. I didn't know any difference, and it didn't matter. I wished my family would go to church. I would feel God's Presence everywhere and His peace. *Love had marked me with the peace of His Presence.*

Christmas was a wonderful time, and I loved to gaze at the baby figure in the crèche and listen to Christmas music celebrating His goodness. *Love had marked me with joy, His goodness, and His abundance.*

Unfortunately, because of a background of ongoing emotional and sexual abuse and neglect, I was bathed in shame and a sense of worthlessness. There were many truly good and lovely things in our family, but these did not dislodge the ongoing unrelenting shame and insecurity that plagued me. It wasn't that I just *felt* shame, I *was* shame. Shame had been imprinted on my heart and identity. I internalized the lie that since I wasn't intrinsically valuable, my value was based upon performance. Being raised in a liberal academic family, Jesus as God and Lord was not valued, but rather disdained. I would sneak reading my Bible, but would feel ashamed for wanting to read it at the same time. Even here *Love had marked me with a hunger for Truth and His Word.*

Making Vows

At age seven, I distinctly remember thinking, "If this is the name of the game, I will do the hardest thing possible." For me, the hardest, most noble thing I knew was to become a doctor, and I vowed I would do just that. The thing with vows is that they set in motion all sorts of damaging psychological, emotional, and spiritual dynamics. That is why the Word of God says to "make no oath at all" (Matthew 5:33-37). That vow set in motion a human doing/human striving program for significance. I didn't consult the God Who had been revealing Himself to me so early on. I was starting to forget about Him, because my heart was hardening. With ongoing family destruction and chaos, I rebelled against Him and chose to trust in myself and my own miserable self-effort. To make matters worse, I was cruelly ostracized by peers.

Jesus, nevertheless, relentlessly continued to pursue me. *Love had marked me with a consciousness of His relentless pursuit.*

However, my hardened, foolish heart was not receptive, and I honestly found this more of an annoyance at best. As I grew into my teens, our family and most everything that mattered to me disintegrated, and I was flat out enraged at this so-called good and powerful God. He seemed either uncaring and clueless or impotent and irrelevant, because in my mind, He "let" horrible things happen. But like most of the pain I had endured, I stuffed all that rage. I really had to during that time in order to survive.

The inner vow I made drove me throughout all my school years. I worked very hard, and I did perform. I was driven, miserable, insecure, tormented, confused, and angry. But I did do very well academically. *Love had marked me with intelligence, favor, and the willingness to work hard.*

I was Phi Beta Kappa, of course, and went to an Ivy-League medical school, and an Ivy-League residency program. I did a chief residency, and actually became the residency director. I moonlighted on the side, often working one hundred hours a week (yeah, scary, I know).

Private Chaos, Personal Epiphany

During all this time, my personal life (as much as there was time for one) was a mess. I married the man I had been with for ten years, ignoring my family's pleas against it and the still small nagging voice inside. I foolishly silenced all those voices and said, "I am going to *make* this work!" Well, not surprisingly, I wasn't able to make the marriage work, and one year later, I cut my losses and filed for divorce – something I thought I would never do. After that I spiraled into one destructive relationship after the next. *Love had marked me with undeserved protection during sin and my foolishness.*

I also started having overwhelming, tangible, demonically tormenting flashbacks of sexual abuse.

My beautiful sister, who had come to know the Lord, kept telling me about Him. She was loving and safe and did not have an agenda, except the best for me. I am still eternally, endlessly, and forever grateful for her. *Love had marked me with an encounter with non-judgmental love and "Jesus in a sister suit."*

Holy Spirit had been pursuing me hard, and finally, one day, after making rounds in the ICU, I gave it up. I went into the residents quarters, knelt down, and told the Lord that He could have me. What a favor I was doing for God – so ridiculous! But God is *so good*; it was as if He was saying, "Great, that works for Me!" There were no visitations, heavens parting, or angelic music. I did not feel much of anything, but I did mean it. *Love had marked me with forgiveness and mercy.*

I was on a new mission. I set about the whole Christian thing as a good student, searching out the Bible. I felt overwhelmingly hopeless and despondent, but, as a good student, I would study and confess scripture. The problem was I was truly heavily spiritually oppressed. It took me a year to figure out what the "Lamb of God" meant. I would go to church on Sundays, but I didn't trust or really "get" all of "those people." They were really nice, but I just didn't have a grid for any of it. I know many of you can relate. I remember the pastor's wife invited me for Sunday dinners, and I could see that she was so very concerned for me but felt helpless. It was kind of freaky. What was she seeing? Hey, I was this big-shot doctor, right? *Love had marked me with an encounter with another person who saw past the facade, saw my pain, and cared.*

But I was still having flashbacks with a lot of demonic torment. I had no clue about my authority in Christ or about much of anything else spiritually, for that matter. It didn't occur to me to reach out for help. I remember it got so bad that I would go to the church building in the middle of the night and sit on the front steps just to get a little relief. I started having random visions of God helping me, but they really made no sense to me. I remember one time I was worshiping in my apartment and heaven broke through so tangibly and unexpectedly that it freaked me out and I totally shut it down – silly me! I was really, *really* clueless, but God was walking me out. *Love had marked me with hope and deliverance by His strong, masterful, steady arm.*

I finally came to the end of myself when it came to men and the series of destructive relationships I had been sucked into. One day I came home and threw myself on my bed and told the Lord, "I clearly have no judgment when it comes to men. If I am supposed to be married, You pick him; otherwise, I don't want one!" And I meant it – from the depths of my being. I had finally laid down this idol. *Love had marked me with the blessing of coming to the end of myself. Love had marked me with His patience, His faithfulness, His masterfulness, and His strength. God is so awesome!*

Two weeks later, completely supernaturally, I met an amazing naval officer through a dating service I had signed up for on a lark. Three months later, much to the initial alarm of my mother, Brian and I were married. And we have had a wonderful miracle (for me) of a marriage for going on twenty-two years to (the publishing) date. During that time, Brian has loved me, protected me, comforted me, supported me, and put up with me when he hasn't always understood me. He has faithfully pitched in to help with the kids and the house. He's sacrificed for the kids and me again and again. He's laughed with me and traveled with me (or me with him) and hung out with me. He has served alongside me and served me. He is a truly wonderful dad. And what a handsome Tomcat fighter guy! I have no words sufficient for this amazing gift to me!

So, yes, thank you, Brian, and thank You, Jesus! *Love had marked me with restoration and the fulfillment of so many of the deepest desires of my heart.*

Transition

I went into full-time internal medicine practice. I was a very competent and conscientious, if anal-retentive, physician (an excellent quality in internal medicine). I truly cared about my patients. However, the realities and trappings around the practice were a huge burden. At some point I realized that although it was an honorable thing and something that had come at a huge cost, medicine was something that just didn't fit me or me it. After a long struggle with bare bones living to pay off all those heavy-duty Ivy-League-level loans, I finally retired from full-time medical practice to pursue my heart's dream: to raise amazing, happy, and thriving kids inside a healthy, wonderful marriage. I found myself pregnant with my first child, Veronica. *Love had marked me again with restoration and as the God of the impossible.*

We started the naval career dance of moving every two years or so and zipping back and forth across the country.

I developed an insatiable hunger for the Word of God and spent hour after hour after hour studying and unpacking the Word of God, listening to teachings, and studying them out for myself. The same God that I had encountered and later rebelled against and ran from put me in an intense program of healing and mind renewal. I went to Christian counseling. I was filled with the Spirit. I went to conferences and trainings and so on. *Love had marked me with His healing, restoration, and preparation.*

My second child, Rachel, was born. *Love had marked me with joy and laughter.*

I started doing small groups and teaching at church, and I continued to grow more and more. During the Iraqi War, Brian was deployed for months at a time and then for an entire year (before the days of Skype). I felt very vulnerable and alone with two very young children. I pressed into the Lord and my church community even more. I also served doing this and that. During this time the Lord was intensively healing my heart. *Love had marked me with deliverance, healing, and His keeping power.*

Rare & Beautiful Treasures

One night I had a vision. God showed me as my adult self in my old house walking in the upper floors of a beautiful three-story home. But something was *terribly* wrong and menacing. I could not put my finger on it. I was drawn to the lowest basement floor, and there was a room that I knew to be a little girl's room. I did *not* want to go in there. But I was drawn. As I opened the door to the room, painted in light pink, there was the scene of a bomb that had gone off. Dust was settling. There was a large pile of rubble in the middle of the room with blood splattered here and there. On top of the rubble were the remains of a little girl - nothing was really left except a face with no mouth and two large blues eyes, tears streaming down them. In the closet was the perpetrator laughing. Ahhhh! I screamed, slammed the door, and ran up the stairs. I bolted up out of my sleep screaming. I knew this little girl was me. I was a wreck for three days – feeling like that decimated little child with no mouth. My husband was on deployment, and it was all I could do to take care of my little girls. I clung onto Jesus. On the third day (the irony not lost on me), Pappa spoke, "Catherine, what do you see?" I looked with my spiritual eyes and saw the same room again. But this time it was *completely spotless*. Every evil and destructive thing was gone. The room was empty, pink, and so beautifully clean and shiny. As I continued to look, the glory of the Lord grew, engulfing everything. And then He said to me, "Let's fill it with beautiful things!" And He has been filling me and filling my life with beautiful things ever since. Thank You, Jesus!!!

By wisdom a house is built, and through understanding it is established; through knowledge its rooms are filled with rare and beautiful treasures. (Proverbs 24:3-4 NIV)

And provide for those who grieve in Zion — to bestow on them a crown of beauty instead of ashes, the oil of joy instead of mourning, and a garment of praise instead of a spirit of despair. They will be called oaks of righteousness, a planting of the Lord for the display of his splendor. (Isaiah 61:3 NIV)

Love had marked me with resurrection power, beauty for ashes, and rare and beautiful treasures.

The Call

Brian came home from war, and shortly after that I found out I was pregnant with the boy we had prayed for. As I was praising God, the Lord whispered in my left ear, "This one will be a preacher!" *Love had marked me again with recompense, joy, and promise!*

With multiple moves and serving in various capacities, we ended up in Colorado on a word from God. It was there that I met up with Schlyce Jimenez while at Bible college. It was a divine appointment and lifelong partnership and friendship. Schlyce is one of the most authentic, transparent, and powerful people I have ever met. She has poured her life out before the Lord. She has made mistakes that have cost her dearly. She never has swept them under the carpet to protect her reputation before men. She has courageously owned them and done her best to clean them up. She has suffered betrayals, loss, and lean times, but has kept going when others would have quit and have quit a long time ago. She has one of the most beautiful, intimate relationships with the Lord I have ever seen. As an anointed power-packed prophet and apostle, she has trained me, equipped me, imparted into me, corrected me, believed in me, given me opportunities, and encouraged my family and me. She saw me when no one else did. And she has done this for many others. I am very grateful for her and for the opportunity to serve with her. *Love had marked me with a mentor, purpose, and promise, and a close friend.*

During those early years with Schlyce, God called me into full-time ministry – what a shocker! Ministers, not to mention Christians, were the same people I was brought up to believe were cracked! The problem was that my mind and heart were still in performance mode. I switched from performing in school to performing in medicine, and then performing as a mother and wife, and finally, to performing as a minister. I knew I had a big assignment. Early on He told me I was a prophet and apostle as well as a teacher, before I really knew what those were. I kept thinking of stained glass windows. *Love had marked me with a high call, gifts, and anointings and the honor of releasing that in others.*

The problem was that I was subconsciously getting my identity from my call, my gifts, my anointing, and my assignments. It was a way of being that God was going to demolish.

The Demolition

And let's be clear, the demolishment was excruciating. He loving-ly turned me inside out, methodically and masterfully, healing my heart and mind in painful stages. He knows what we can handle!

He kept me on a shelf for years, hidden or with small assignments, and reigned me in until He could get my heart healed enough and my mind renewed enough to be happy and fulfilled just being His beloved child. That took a while. That was safety for me, and that was safety for others! *Love had marked me with humility, patience, faithfulness, and endurance.*

First and foremost, God is a jealous God – *for* us. If anything comes before Him, that is an idol, and that is an area where we are standing on shakable and dangerous ground. The only totally safe place to be is His first, and because He is Love, He richly gives us all things to enjoy (1 Timothy 6:17). He is jealous to be the Source of all things. And guess what, He really is!!!

Learning to be happy and fulfilled just being His beloved kid went down hard. It sounds pretty easy, but if you have no grid for that, it feels like death and incredible rejection. This is particularly true when you are not promoted and released when you think you are ready, watching person after person being promoted and released before you.

But God knows what He is doing! And He loves us way too much to leave us in the deathtrap of getting our identity from anyone or anything else other than Him. *Love had marked me with purity, His masterfulness, dependency, royalty, and daughtership.*

In the Meantime

In the meantime, He continued to restore so many areas, including my family. My mother came to the Lord in a glorious supernatural way, and He restored our broken relationship. He also healed places that were broken with my sister, and helped me reconcile and make peace with my father, really loving him exactly where he was at. *Love had marked me with the restoration of my family line.*

> YOU HAVE BEEN MARKED BY LOVE AND RELEASED TO MAKE A MARK THAT LOOKS UNIQUELY LIKE HIM THROUGH YOU.

I continued to be faithful sowing into others' amazing ministries, with all the ups and downs of starting an apostolic/prophetic ministry. I was being trained and imparted into. *Love had marked me with preparation and impartation.*

When He finally told me it was time to launch my own separate ministry, the thing that had been my deep-seated idol – long laid down – I was honored, but I was not reveling in it. Truly He is my revelry and my Source. Nothing satisfies and undergirds and can even come close to Him. I know what it is like to be dead and made alive in so many areas. I really know Him, because I am so known by Him. *Love had marked me with intimacy and the knowledge of Love Himself.*

I have been marked by His Love and released to make a mark that looks uniquely like Him through me.

And that is my heart's cry for you!

10.
FINAL
THOUGHTS

And so we are back to where we started. You have been marked by Love.

You are His. You are Love's. And He wants to be your Source of all good things!

My heart is that you go deep, deep, deep into Love, Himself. Let Him reveal exactly Who He is and who He created you to be.

You are marked by Love, to make your mark on a lost and dying world starving for Love!

Appendix A

All Things – a Bountiful Meditation Project

Love swallowed all of the cosmos up in Himself. He is, in fact, drawing *all things* to Himself.

That is why you can do *all things* through Him, Who provides the strength (Philippians 4:13).

That's why *all things* are possible with Him (Matthew 19:26; Mark 10:27).

That *all things* work together for our good (Romans 8:28).

Seeking the kingdom first, *all things* will be added (Matthew 6:33).

All things have been committed to Jesus by Pappa (Matthew 11:27; Luke 10:22).

Through Him *all things* were made; without Him nothing was made that has been made (John 1:3).

Pappa put *all things* under His power (John 13:13).

Holy Spirit will teach us *all things* and will remind us of everything Jesus has said (John 14:26; 1 John 2:27).

His hand has made *all things* (Isaiah 66:1,2).

Pappa, Who did not spare His own Son, but gave him up for us all – how will He not also, along with Him, graciously give us *all things* (Romans 8:32)?

For from him and through him and for him are *all things* (Romans 11:36).

The Spirit searches *all things*, even the deep things of God (1 Corinthians 2:10).

Pappa is where *all things* came from and for whom we live; and Jesus Christ, through Whom *all things* came and through whom we live (1 Corinthians 8:6).

He is able to bless us abundantly, so that in *all things* at all times, having all that we need, we will abound in every good work (2 Corinthians 9:8).

He made known to us the mystery of His will according to His good pleasure, which He purposed in Christ, to bring unity to *all things* in heaven and on earth under Christ (Ephesians 1:9-11).

Pappa placed *all things* under Jesus's feet and appointed Jesus to be head over everything for the church (Ephesians 1:22).

The mystery of the boundless riches of Christ, Who created *all things* (Ephesians 3:8-9).

I wanted to quote this mother of *"all things"* scriptures straight up. Check this out!

> *For in him all things were created: things in heaven and on earth, visible and invisible, whether thrones or powers or rulers or authorities; all things have been created through him and for him. He is before all things, and in him all things hold together. And he is the head of the body, the church; he is the beginning and the firstborn from among the dead, so that in everything he might have the supremacy. For God was pleased to have all his fullness dwell in him, and through him to reconcile to himself all things, whether things on earth or things in heaven, by making peace through his blood, shed on the cross. (Colossians 1:16-20 NIV)*

God's Final word was His Son. He has spoken to us by His Son, Whom He appointed heir of *all things*, and through Whom also He made the universe. The Son is the radiance of God's glory and the exact representation of His being, sustaining *all things* by His powerful word (Hebrews 1:2-3 NIV).

And finally in the Revelations to cap it all off:

> *He is worthy to receive glory and honor and power, for He cre-ated all things, and by His will they were created and have their being (Revelation 4:11).*

APPENDIX B

"How to Hear God's Voice" by Mark Virkler

She had done it again! Instead of coming straight home from school like she was supposed to, she had gone to her friend's house. Without permission. Without our knowledge. Without doing her chores. With a ministering household that included remnants of three struggling families plus our own toddler and newborn, my wife simply couldn't handle all the work on her own. Everyone had to pull their own weight. Everyone had age-appropriate tasks they were expected to complete. At fourteen, Rachel and her younger brother were living with us while her parents tried to overcome lifestyle patterns that had resulted in the children running away to escape the dysfunction. I felt sorry for Rachel, but honestly my wife was my greatest concern.

Now Rachel had ditched her chores to spend time with her friends. It wasn't the first time, but if I had anything to say about it, it would be the last. I intended to lay down the law when she got home and make it very clear that if she was going to live under my roof, she would obey my rules.

But she wasn't home yet. And I had recently been learning to hear God's voice more clearly. Maybe I should try to see if I could hear anything from Him about the situation. Maybe He could give me a way to get her to do what she was supposed to (i.e., what I wanted her to do). So I went to my office and reviewed what the Lord had been teaching me from Habakkuk 2:1,2:

> *I will stand on my guard post... and station myself on the rampart; And I will keep watch to see what He will speak to me. Then the Lord answered me and said, "Record the vision." Habakkuk said, "I will stand on my guard post..." (Hab. 2:1).*

| **The first key to hearing God's voice is to go to a quiet place and still our own thoughts and emotions.** |

Psalm 46:10 encourages us to be still, let go, cease striving, and know that He is God. In Psalm 37:7 we are called to "be still before the Lord and wait patiently for Him." There is a deep inner knowing in our spirits that each of us can experience when we quiet our flesh and our minds. Practicing the art of biblical meditation helps silence the outer noise and distractions clamoring for our attention.

I didn't have a guard post but, I did have an office, so I went there to quiet my temper and my mind. Loving God through a quiet worship song is one very effective way to become still. In 2 Kings 3, Elisha needed a word from the Lord, so he said, "Bring me a minstrel," and as the minstrel played, the Lord spoke. I have found that playing a worship song on my autoharp is the quickest way for me to come to stillness. I need to choose my song carefully; boisterous songs of praise do not bring me to stillness, but rather gentle songs that express my love and worship. And it isn't enough just to sing the song into the cosmos. I come into the Lord's presence most quickly and easily when I use my godly imagination to see the truth that He is right here with me and I sing my songs to Him, personally.

"I will keep watch to see," said the prophet. To receive the pure word of God, it is very important that my heart be properly focused as I become still, because my focus is the source of the intuitive flow. If I fix my eyes upon Jesus (Heb. 12:2), the intuitive flow comes from Jesus. But if I fix my gaze upon some desire of my heart, the intuitive flow comes out of that desire. To have a pure flow I must become still and carefully fix my eyes upon Jesus. Quietly worshiping the King and receiving out of the stillness that follows quite easily accomplishes this.

So I used | **the second key to hearing God's voice: As you pray, fix the eyes of your heart upon Jesus, seeing in the Spirit the dreams and visions of Almighty God.** | Habakkuk was actually looking for vision as he prayed. He opened the eyes of his heart and looked into the spirit world to see what God wanted to show him.

God has always spoken through dreams and visions, and He specifically said that they would come to those upon whom the Holy Spirit is poured out (Acts 2:1-4, 17).

Being a logical, rational person, observable facts that could be veri-
fied by my physical senses were the foundations of my life, including
my spiritual life. I had never thought of opening the eyes of my heart
and looking for vision. However, I have come to believe that this is
exactly what God wants me to do. He gave me eyes in my heart to
see in the spirit the vision and movement of Almighty God. There is
an active spirit world all around us, full of angels, demons, the Holy
Spirit, the omnipresent Father, and His omnipresent Son, Jesus. The
only reasons for me not to see this reality are unbelief or lack of
knowledge.

In his sermon in Acts 2:25, Peter refers to King David's statement:

> *I saw the Lord always in my presence; for He is at my right*
> *hand, so that I will not be shaken.*

The original psalm makes it clear that this was a decision of David's,
not a constant supernatural visitation: "I have set (literally, I have
placed) the Lord continually before me; because He is at my right
hand, I will not be shaken" (Ps. 16:8). Because David knew that the
Lord was always with him, he determined in his spirit to see that
truth with the eyes of his heart as he went through life, knowing that
this would keep his faith strong.

In order to see, we must look. Daniel saw a vision in his mind and
said, "I was looking...I kept looking...I kept looking" (Dan. 7:2, 9,
13). As I pray, I look for Jesus, and I watch as He speaks to me, doing

and saying the things that are on His heart. Many Christians will find that if they will only look, they will see. Jesus is Emmanuel, God with us (Matt. 1:23). It is as simple as that. You can see Christ present with you because Christ is present with you. In fact, the vision may come so easily that you will be tempted to reject it, thinking that it is just you. But if you persist in recording these visions, your doubt will soon be overcome by faith as you recognize that the content of them could only be birthed in Almighty God. Jesus demonstrated the ability of living out of constant contact with God, declaring that He did nothing on His own initiative, but only what He saw the Father doing and heard the Father saying (Jn. 5:19,20,30).

What an incredible way to live! Is it possible for us to live out of divine initiative as Jesus did? Yes! We must simply fix our eyes upon Jesus. The veil has been torn, giving access into the immediate presence of God, and He calls us to draw near (Lk. 23:45; Heb. 10:19-22). "I pray that the eyes of your heart may be enlightened" (Ephesians 1:18 NASB).

When I had quieted my heart enough that I was able to picture Jesus without the distractions of my own ideas and plans, I was able to "keep watch to see what He will speak to me." I wrote down my question: "Lord, what should I do about Rachel?"

Immediately the thought came to me, "She is insecure." Well, that certainly wasn't my thought! Her behavior looked like rebellion to me, not insecurity.

But like Habakkuk, I was coming to know the sound of God speaking to me (Hab. 2:2). Elijah described it as a still, small voice (I Kings 19:12). I had previously listened for an inner audible voice, and God does speak that way at times. However, I have found that usually, God's voice comes as spontaneous thoughts, visions, feelings, or impressions.

For example, haven't you been driving down the road and had a thought come to you to pray for a certain person? Didn't you believe it was God telling you to pray? What did God's voice sound like? Was it an audible voice, or was it a spontaneous thought that lit upon your mind?

Experience indicates that we perceive spirit-level communication as spontaneous thoughts, impressions, and visions, and Scripture confirms this in many ways. For example, one definition of *paga*, a Hebrew word for intercession, is "a chance encounter or an accidental intersecting." When God lays people on our hearts, He does it through *paga*, a chance-encounter thought "accidentally" intersecting our minds.

So | **the third key to hearing God's voice is recognizing that God's voice in your heart often sounds like a flow of spontaneous thoughts.**| Therefore, when I want to hear from God, I tune to chance-encounter or spontaneous thoughts.

Finally, God told Habakkuk to record the vision (Hab. 2:2). This was not an isolated command. The Scriptures record many examples of individual's prayers and God's replies, such as the Psalms, many of the prophets, and Revelation. I have found that obeying this final principle amplified my confidence in my ability to hear God's voice so that I could finally make living out of His initiatives a way of life.

|**The fourth key, two-way journaling or the writing out of your prayers and God's answers, brings great freedom in hearing God's voice.** | I have found two-way journaling to be a fabulous catalyst for clearly discerning God's inner, spontaneous flow, because as I journal I am able to write in faith for long periods of time, simply believing it is God. I know that what I believe I have received from God must be tested. However, testing involves doubt and doubt blocks divine communication, so I do not want to test while I am trying to receive. (See James 1:5-8.) With journaling, I can receive in faith, knowing that when the flow has ended I can test and examine it carefully.

So I wrote down what I believed He had said: "She is insecure." But the Lord wasn't done.

I continued to write the spontaneous thoughts that came to me: "Love her unconditionally. She is flesh of your flesh and bone of your bone."

My mind immediately objected: "She is not flesh of my flesh. She is not related to me at all – she is a foster child, just living in my home temporarily." It was definitely time to test this "word from the

Lord"! There are three possible sources of thoughts in our minds: ourselves, satan and the Holy Spirit. It was obvious that the words in my journal did not come from my own mind – I certainly didn't see her as insecure or flesh of my flesh. And I sincerely doubted that satan would encourage me to love anyone unconditionally!

Okay, it was starting to look like I might have actually received counsel from the Lord. It was consistent with the names and character of God as revealed in the Scripture, and totally contrary to the names and character of the enemy. So that meant that I was hearing from the Lord, and He wanted me to see the situation in a different light. Rachel was my daughter – part of my family not by blood but by the hand of God Himself. The chaos of her birth home had created deep insecurity about her worthiness to be loved by anyone, including me and including God. Only the unconditional love of the Lord expressed through an imperfect human would reach her heart.

But there was still one more test I needed to perform before I would have absolute confidence that this was truly God's word to me: I needed confirmation from someone else whose spiritual discernment I trusted. So I went to my wife and shared what I had received. I knew if I could get her validation, especially since she was the one most wronged in the situation, then I could say, at least to myself, "Thus sayeth the Lord." Needless to say, Patti immediately and without question confirmed that the Lord had spoken to me. My entire planned lecture was forgotten. I returned to my office anxious to hear more. As the Lord planted a new, supernatural love for Rachel within me, He showed me what to say and how to say it to not only address the current issue of household responsibility, but the deeper issues of love and acceptance and worthiness.

Rachel and her brother remained as part of our family for another two years, giving us many opportunities to demonstrate and teach about the Father's love, planting spiritual seeds in thirsty soil. We weren't perfect and we didn't solve all of her issues, but because I had learned to listen to the Lord, we were able to avoid creating more brokenness and separation.

The four simple keys that the Lord showed me from Habakkuk have been used by people of all ages, from four to a hundred and four, from every continent, culture and denomination, to break through into intimate two-way conversations with their loving Father and dearest Friend. Omitting any one of the keys will prevent you from receiving all He wants to say to you. The order of the keys is not important, just that you use them all. Embracing all four, by faith, can change your life. Simply quiet yourself down, tune to spontaneity, look for vision, and journal. He is waiting to meet you there.

You will be amazed when you journal! Doubt may hinder you at first, but throw it off, reminding yourself that it is a biblical concept and that God is present, speaking to His children. Relax. When we cease our labors and enter His rest, God is free to flow (Heb. 4:10).

Why not try it for yourself, right now? Sit back comfortably, take out your pen and paper, and smile. Turn your attention toward the Lord in praise and worship, seeking His face. Many people have found the music and visionary prayer called "A Stroll Along the Sea of Galilee" helpful in getting them started. You can listen to it and download it free at www.CWGMinistries.org/Galilee.

After you write your question to Him, become still, fixing your gaze on Jesus. You will suddenly have a very good thought. Don't doubt it; simply write it down. Later, as you read your journaling you too, will be blessed to discover that you are indeed dialoguing with God. If you wonder if it is really the Lord speaking to you, share it with your spouse or a friend. Their input will encourage your faith and strengthen your commitment to spend time getting to know the Lover of your soul more intimately than you ever dreamed possible.

Is It Really God?

Five ways to be sure what you're hearing is from Him:

1) **Test the Origin** (1 Jn. 4:1) – Thoughts from our own minds are progressive, with one thought leading to the next, however tangentially. Thoughts from the spirit world are spontaneous. The Hebrew word for true prophecy is *naba*, which literally means "to bubble up," whereas false prophecy is *ziyd* meaning "to boil up." True words from the Lord will bubble up from our innermost being; we don't need to cook them up ourselves.

2) **Compare It to Biblical Principles** – God will never say something to you personally which is contrary to His universal revelation as expressed in the Scriptures. If the Bible clearly states that something is a sin, no amount of journaling can make it right. Much of what you journal about will not be specifically addressed in the Bible, however, so an understanding of biblical principles is also needed.

3) **Compare It to the Names and Character of God as Revealed in the Bible** – Anything God says to you will be in harmony with His essential nature. Journaling will help you get to know God personally, but knowing what the Bible says about Him will help you discern what words are from Him. Make sure the tenor of your journaling lines up with the character of God as described in the names of the Father, Son, and Holy Spirit.

4) **Test the Fruit** (Matt. 7:15-20) – What effect does what you are hearing have on your soul and your spirit? Words from the Lord will quicken your faith and increase your love, peace, and joy. They will stimulate a sense of humility within you as you become more aware of Who God is and who you are. On the other hand, any words you receive which cause you to fear or doubt, which bring you into confusion or anxiety, or which stroke your ego (especially if you hear something that is "just for you alone, no one else is worthy") must be immediately rebuked and rejected as lies of the enemy.

5) **Share It with Your Spiritual Counselors** (Prov. 11:14) – We are members of a Body! A cord of three strands is not easily broken and

God's intention has always been for us to grow together. Nothing will increase your faith in your ability to hear from God like having it confirmed by two or three other people! Share it with your spouse, your parents, your friends, your elder, your group leader; even your grown children can be your sounding board. They don't need to be perfect or super-spiritual; they just need to love you, be committed to being available to you, have a solid biblical orientation, and most importantly, they must also willingly and easily receive counsel. Avoid the authoritarian who insists that because of their standing in the church or with God, they no longer need to listen to others. Find two or three people and let them confirm that you are hearing from God!

The book *4 Keys to Hearing God's Voice* is available at www.CWG-Ministries.org.

Appendix C
Two-Way Journaling Sample

"What About Your Marked By Love Audience?"

CATHERINE: Pappa, thank You for Your tenderness and passion for this *Marked by Love* project. This is Your project. You have been so passionate and relentless in seeing to it that it is launched and launched well. Even as I was clueless, You placed out the breadcrumbs for me and my team to follow, and here we are. Thank you for bringing all this together. Your heart for your people is too great for words! But I know you have lots to say to your people. Pappa, what do you want your *Marked by Love* audience to know?

LOVE: Catherine, My Dove, you have My heart and you are sharing it well. I have prepared you as My mouthpiece and I will continue to speak through you. Thank you for being bold and obedient to step out. Isn't it fun on the water? We will continue to have many adventures together. You love well, and I love loving through you! Buckle up, We have just begun!

My Precious one (that's YOU!), I have said in My Word how I longed to gather you together as a mother hen gathers her chicks, and you have said, "Yes." How My heart swells with pride – YOU are Mine! You have no idea the effect you have on Me. How I long for you to quit getting tripped up on the stains you see in yourself and fix your gaze upon Me and continue in that gaze. You have nothing to fear. I will help you, and I AM so glad to do so.

Some of my children are afraid because they feel shame. But, oh, My Beloved one, do you not know that I cleansed you from *all shame*? Do you not know that you shine, *oh-so brightly*? The stains you see are a lie. I never made you for lies, but I made you for the Truth of My love. There is nothing ugly about you! I made you beautiful, powerful, and joyful, and a carrier of My Presence. I made you to be transformed by My love and carry that transformation wherever you go. I never fail. In the places that have seemed that I failed, even in very profound ways, I am greater than the depths of any failure.

I hung on that cross just for you – intimately, extravagantly, irreversibly – just for you. I sought you out and still seek you in the places where your heart has been shut off, shut down, and where you have shut Me out – even if you don't know it. I MADE you for My victorious Kingdom. I made you just like Me – in every detail. I left nothing out. I will help you get there from here. And like My Daughter says, I AM masterfully good at My job!

CATHERINE: Thank You, Pappa. What else do you want your child to know?

LOVE: I AM an all-inclusive God. What I mean by that is that I included everyone ever born in the deal when I hung on that cross and died for the whole world. My salvation is a starting point, ending point, and everything in between. The human race starts with Me, and while they may not know Me or they may flat out reject Me, I never rescind My offer to wake up to. My people perish for lack of knowledge, and what they really need to know is Me. My Love will either bring the ecstatic joy or fiery torment depending upon the state of the heart. But there is no place that I AM not present, and there is no place that I deny Myself and the nature of Myself as Love and My faithfulness. You, even in the midst of frank sin, even if it is "only" unbelief, are not excluded from My best. I make no second-rate offers. YOU are not second-rate. You are "good enough" because I said so. I offered My Son for you and have never felt I got the short end of the stick. You were worth it. You are worth it. Never forget your value. You can look straight into My eyes and see My love and see yourself through My eyes. Keep staring. I know it is intense. But My passion for you is intense. I will give you the grace to keep gazing longer and longer into My eyes. I AM transforming you, and you are beautiful and you are powerful. You are being transformed by My love even now. Do not draw back. If you do, just ask for My help not to. I will help you. I want you standing tall, proud, and confident in Me and not in yourselves. YOU are called to release My love wherever you go. But receive it first. I will help you. I will

ALWAYS help you wherever you get stuck. Look to Me.

CATHERINE: Wow, Pappa - pretty intense. Can you help your child see your playful fun light side as well?

LOVE: HAHAHAHAHA! I thought you'd never ask. I LOVE to have fun. I love to play. I love to have My kids, yes, even and particularly My "adult" kids, play. HAHAHAHA! See I AM tickling you. Don't worry – I know when to stop. But some of my kids are WAY too serious! Don't you know that I have *everything* taken care of? I AM aware of the seriousness of the world's problems – more than you. I AM aware of your problems. But didn't you hear? I overcame the world! Taking time out to play with Me and allowing yourself to relax and play is such a testimony to My sovereign mastery over the world, time, and space, and even over death. I keep you safe and protect you – you can afford to play. I LOVE to laugh! HAHAHA-HAHA! What the enemy has thrown against you is so ridiculously stupid, I have to laugh. But I don't laugh at what it has cost you. And when he happens to get his sucker punches through, I AM there to help. I AM there to heal and to resurrect and recompense. But seeing your "problems" from My perspective: HAHAHAHAHAHA! See, you can afford to cheer up because I have already overcome what you are facing. See, My Beloved powerful one, you laughing with Me from My perspective shrinks the problems down to joke-level – it totally demoralizes the one who has come to demoralize you. Look how huge I AM – HAHAHAHAHAHA! Look how huge I have made you to be – HAHAHAHAHAHA! Let us laugh together because My joy is your strength HAHAHAHAHA!

CATHERINE: I see you, dear reader, as a little child – Love is playfully messing up your hair and laughing. You are playfully messing up His hair, and you both are laughing. Hahahaha! Pappa, You are such a fun God! What a relief from all the heavy!

LOVE: Yes, that is something I want to address. Many of My kids feel that being responsible means they are to carry the cares of the world. Nothing could be further from the truth. My kids were never built to carry burdens. I AM the carrier of the heaviest parts of life's burdens. The lie is that when they don't carry that heaviness, they are being irresponsible. It is a lie from the pit of hell, and that lie is breaking down My body. I meant My body to travel light. I get to do all the heavy lifting. That is not only My willingness, but My prerogative. Make sure, My beloved one, that you are handing Me the burdens of your cares every day throughout the day. I will help you. I will help you, not only walk lightly and freely, but I will give you dancing feet and the rhythm to go with it if you need it. I will help you love yourself and others deeply. You can become famous for My love. I will love through you. And you will draw others to Me, just by the way you carry yourself.

CATHERINE: Pappa, any final words?

LOVE: Oh yes, I always have a lot to say – sometimes with no words. I AM taking you on a journey to discover Me more deeply. I will use the pages of this book to do so, and you will start to encounter Me more and more. Hahaha! Oh the fun we are going to have together.

And there is always more. We'll start from where you are, and keep going together. And do not be fooled. This will not only be fun, but also oh so powerful. My love is a force that never fails because it is Me. Me transforming you into My image will be breathtaking. So let's go forward together; I will help you! I love you more than you can take in. BAM, and yes, I have marked you with My Love!!!

APPENDIX D

I Want to Know I Am Saved!

I am in no way proposing that this short summary can remotely begin to do justice to the finished work of the cross (are you kidding?). But if you want to know you are saved, here are some glorious highlights. I will trust Holy Spirit to unpack His Word and revelation of that Word.

Salvation was God's idea and fulfilled plan before humankind existed (Revelation 13:8). Before there was a problem, the Godhead masterminded and provided the solution in the person of Christ. Love had you covered before there was even a "you" to cover! In that, Christ died for the sins of the entire world, or in other scriptures "all men" (John 1:29; 1 John 2:2; 1 Corinthians 15:22; 2 Corinthians 5:14-15,19; Romans 6:10; Hebrews 2:9). This is an objective reality whether or not humankind chooses to participate subjectively. To experience that reality requires faith, which God supplies.

I love how John Crowder puts in his *Cosmos Reborn* book[1]:

> *My faith doesn't create Reality. It simply trusts in Reality. And it is in the midst of faith that Reality manifests.*

---

[1] J. Crowder, Cosmos Reborn: Happy Theology on The New Creation (Marylhurst, Sons of Thunder)

If you want to grapple with and savor this mystery, I highly recommend you read John Crowder's book, which will challenge many preconceived notions that you may have thought were sacred cow no-brainers. It is good to be vigorously challenged with what we believe and why we believe it. We are stronger and better for it, even if the end point is that it all doesn't fit in the neat little boxes we tend to like. And if there is disagreement – even vehement disagreement – no problem, let's just agree to love one another even as we disagree. Love is the main thing and what we are supposed to be *famous* for! Love reveals Himself, but at the end of the day He is fabulously mysterious and we can trust in His goodness in all the places that we do not have it figured out. We can also trust in His mercy for all the places that our theological ducks are out of order. Love covers a multitude of sins – Hallelujah (1 Peter 4:8)!

With this, God hates sin. There is plenty of wrath to be poured out upon this entity that kills, steals, and destroys His precious kids. Love actually condemned the principle of sin itself in the flesh of Christ (Romans 8:3). However, unlike what you may have been taught, God is not the enemy of sinners – He is the Savior of sinners (John 12:47; 1 Timothy 1:15). Now that is good news! But the Word actually says that we were at one time enemies of God but, only in our minds because of sin (Colossians 1:21). Jesus took care of the sin problem that would separate Love from His beloved kids (Romans 8:2; 2 Corinthians 5:21; Luke 2:14). God rescued us and brought us into the kingdom of Christ in Whom we have redemption and forgiveness of sins (Colossians 1:13-14). But humankind chose and still chooses to hide from Him because humans often love darkness more than light (Genesis 3:8; John 3:19). Love is not going to force anyone to live, experience, and enjoy His finished work, even as He is not going to force anyone *not* to.

The work is finished (John 19:30). You add nothing to the equation except being a beloved, forgiven, washed-clean recipient. You are "out" only to the extent that you are asleep or stubbornly resistant to the truth that Christ died for you, as you, for every sin you would ever commit (Romans 6:3-5). If anyone is insistent upon the insanity of hell, God will brokenheartedly accommodate. But I know you are not that foolish, or you would not be reading this book!

So what must you do to be saved?

Believe in the Lord Christ Jesus alone to save you (Acts 4:12; 16:30; Romans 10:9-10, 13)! Receive Holy Spirit's stirring, *His* faith, to believe that Christ died specifically, expressly, and passionately for you, and that His death wiped away every sin you have ever committed or ever will commit (Matthew 26:28; Romans 3:25; Colossians 2:13-15). If you think you have committed the unpardonable sin, realize that your heart's cry to receive forgiveness allows the entry of the very forgiveness that Love longs for you to receive! If you want Love's forgiveness, you have not "blasphemed the Holy Spirit," even if someone told you that you did. That is a demonic lie from the pit of hell.

If sin weighs heavy on you, pour your heart out to Him and receive His forgiveness. Love is HUGE - greater than anything you have done or has been done to you. Let Him wash your conscience of the consciousness of sin with His blood (Hebrews 9:14).

Whatever you say to Love as you come to Him will work. The entity of sin, if not the natural consequences of sin, has already been taken care of. Love can't deny Himself you – you are the object of His passion! If you need some help, say these words out loud so you can hear them, "as is" or in your own way:

> *God, I thank You that You are Love.*
> *I don't really "get" all the love You have for me, but I know I need a Savior!*
> *I realize that only You can save me.*
> *I've messed up! (You can add "a lot" if you feel that way.)*
> *I need Your help!*
> *Help me to believe that, even though you were fully God, You died in the flesh as a man on the cross expressly for me. You rose again on the third day and are seated at the right hand of Father God.*
> *Help me to receive Your forgiveness for every single one of my sins, known and unknown.*
> > *(If you need to confess some sins, do so – get all that mess OUT of you to the only One Who can handle it!)*
> *Help me to forgive myself.*
> *Help me to receive the cleansing of my conscience for the things I have done wrong, by Your blood spilled for me.*
> > *(Take as much time as you need for this).*
> *Heal my heart.*
> *I receive You as my Lord and Savior.*

I want to know You, what it means to be "in You" and to be "one" with You, Jesus.

Help me to know you will never ever leave me or abandon me (Hebrews 13:5) regardless of what I do or do not do. I want to experience the love and all the goodness You have for me, Jesus, Father God, and Holy Spirit.

Help me to grow and keep growing in what all that means and not take on religious burdens that are not mine.

Help me to be transformed into the person you made me to be from glory to glory.

Thank You for Your Love and freedom! In Jesus name, Amen!

Trust Love to faithfully keep you (Jude 1:24) and to help you awaken to all that He is for you (Ephesians 1:17-23)! He is masterful at revealing Himself to you. Trust Him to reveal and unveil the righteous, clean, whole, breathtaking, powerful person He has re-created you to be (2 Corinthians 5:17, 21; 1 Corinthians 15:24; 1 Peter 2:9)! Trust Him to help you walk all that out (John 15:4-5) and to reflect Him more and more (2 Corinthians 5:20; 3:18). Get ready for a wild ,wonderful adventure in Love!

If you need some help with what to do next, feel free to contact us, and we will help where we can. I trust the Lord to lead you exactly where and how you are supposed to go. Praise God – it's party time in heaven and on earth!!!!

ABOUT THE AUTHOR

As an MD in residency, Catherine's life was radically transformed when she had a powerful and personal encounter with Jesus. The Jesus Catherine met that day was the real deal, the same Jesus Who is described in the Bible as a loving, intimate, kind, and accessible miracle worker.

As Catherine developed her relationship with Jesus and grew in her love and trust of Him, He tenderly walked her out of the intense sorrow, suffering, and heavy bondage that had resulted after years of childhood abuse. In the process, Holy Spirit became her very best friend.

Along the way, the Father birthed a burning desire and deep conviction within her heart that He had plans to use her powerfully to help others experience the same Jesus she had come to know so intimately. He would heal and restore others through her in the same way He had healed and restored her. After four years of practice as a board-certified Internist, she retired from medicine to raise her children and wholeheartedly pursue God's call on her life.

In 2007, by divine connection, she met Schlyce Jimenez, Rethink LLC and Emerge School of Transformation's Founder, while attending Charis Bible College. She has been an integral part of Schlyce's life and ministry ever since. She birthed and directed prayer, prophetic, and healing room ministries. In 2011, Catherine spearheaded bringing Sozo, an inner healing ministry and what would become known as Encounter Ministries. Shortly thereafter, she launched and oversaw monthly Encounter Weekends at the ministry"s headquarters, Prayer Mountain, CO, overseeing the Sozo, Prophetic, Healing, Dream Interpretation, Healing Massage, Prophetic Portrait Photography, and Recreational Encounter Teams.

Catherine was officially licensed by Schlyce in February of 2011 and ordained as an Apostle and Prophet by her in February of 2015. Over the years, Catherine has written multiple curricula, teachings, and blogs. She has an anointed, powerful, thorough, and prophetic teaching style. As a powerful prophetic intercessor, who regularly operates in the miraculous, Catherine's prophetic ministry is sought out by leaders and entrepreneurs from around the globe. Her prophetic voice is acutely accurate in speaking forth vision, direction, confirmation, and practical strategic insight into individuals, leaders, organizations, and businesses. She currently serves as the Director of the Emerge Campus School of Transformation program in Woodland Park, CO, which is designed to help students reach their full potential in Christ through transformational teaching, activations, Rapid Mind Renewal sessions, and much more. She also currently directs The Transformation Center.

After years of ministry partnership with Schlyce, Catherine has been released to launch forward globally, fulfilling her heart's desire to touch the entire planet. In 2016 she founded catherinetoon.com and Imprint LLC, a company that is dedicated to restoring wholeness, revealing identity, and releasing destiny to this generation through the unveiling of God's imprint of Love uniquely expressed in every person.

Catherine lives in Colorado Springs, CO, enjoying life with her husband, Brian, and her powerhouse children, Veronica, Rachel, and Robert.

For more information about Catherine Toon and Imprint: www.catherinetoon.com.

CONNECT WITH CATHERINE

Catherine Toon   MEDIA   STORE   ABOUT   BLOG

Author | Prophetic Speaker | Coach

Marked to Make Your Mark.

LEARN MORE

catherinetoon.com

info@catherinetoon.com
markedbylovebook.com

FOLLOW:

Subscribe for fresh daily & weekly inspiration!

 @CatherineToonMD

 catherinetoon

 @CatherineToonMD

 Catherine Toon, MD

 Catherine Toon

Receive daily words of encouragement & weekly videos direct to your inbox.

Sign up @
catherinetoon.com

REQUEST

To request Catherine for speaking engagements:

info@catherinetoon.com

STAY TUNED...

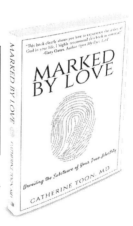

MARKED BY LOVE
e-Course coming Fall 2017!
More info coming soon @
markedbylovebook.com

Catherine's next book is coming:
Payback God's Way!
(release date TBD)

Book & Website Design by Granite Pillar Media, LLC | granitepillarmedia.com